GARCÍA LORCA:
Playwright and Poet

GARCÍA LORCA:

Playwright and Poet

Mildred Adams

GEORGE BRAZILLER
New York

Published in the United States in 1977 by George Braziller, Inc.

For information address the publisher:
George Braziller, Inc.
One Park Avenue, New York 10016

Library of Congress Cataloging in Publication Data
Adams, Mildred
García Lorca: playwright and poet
Bibliography: p.
1. García Lorca, Federico, 1898–1936. 2. Authors,
Spanish—20th century—Biography.
PQ6613.A763Z528 868'.6'209 [B] 77–77561
ISBN 0–8076–0873–4

Printed in the United States of America
First Edition

CONTENTS

ACKNOWLEDGEMENTS

For permission to include material published by them, grateful acknowledgement is made to the following:

W. W. Norton and Co., for permission to quote from *The Poet in New York and Other Poems of Federico García Lorca,* translated by Rolfe Humphries. Copyright © 1940 by W.W. Norton and Co.

Charles Scribner's Sons, for permission to quote from *From Lorca's Theatre: Five Plays,* translated by James Graham-Lujan and Richard O'Connell. Copyright © 1941 Charles Scribner's Sons.

University of Indiana Press, for permission to quote from *Gypsy Ballads* by Federico García Lorca, translated by Rolfe Humphries. Copyright © 1953 by Rolfe Humphries.

FOREWORD

IN THE LAST THREE DECADES Federico García Lorca has become a fixed star in the Spanish literary world, and a favorite poet and dramatist on at least three continents. His poetry forms part of the folk sayings of his people. His plays are presented afresh year after year, by students and by professionals, in Spanish, in English, in French, in German, even in Japanese; they are never "revived" because they have never died. As scenes from *The Public (El Público),* brilliantly presented by students at the University of Texas in 1972, and *Yerma,* displayed to New York audiences amid surrealist surroundings, amply proved, the life in them still holds secrets to be plumbed by new producers.

To try to explain Federico is to evade the fact that he can better be understood in an account of his life and his work than in any analysis by a friend or an enemy; nor can he be comprehended solely by reading what his fellow countrymen write about him. Perhaps for the very reason that they, too, are Spaniards they tend to overlook the important effect on the man and his work of Federico's visits to North and South America. By instinct, being Spaniards, they tend to reject the weight of outside influences on a Spanish writer. His most brilliant, perceptive and premonitory book, *Poet in New York (Poeta en Nueva York),* has been disregarded or disdained by too many Spanish scholars who, not knowing the city, reject the extraordinary clairvoyance of his apocalyptic visions concerning its people. They even fail to realize the importance of his farsighted recognition, in the 1930s, that the Negroes were at once the tragedy and the problem of the metropolis.

Federico was a poet, a dramatist, a seer, and one of the most enchantingly funny and friendly people who ever came to visit and remained to excoriate New York. Like Lope de Vega he was a freak of nature, in that nothing in his background offered a hint of what he would become. The Spanish Civil War made him a martyr to the cause of the Republic, but not—as is too often misstated—a martyr to Communism, with which he had no connection. Four decades after his death, Federico García Lorca is still a name that echoes in books and on playbills, a tragic martyr to Falangist terror, a ghost coming invisible into conversations with his sister, his friends. It has not been easy to recall his earlier image from the past. Myth enters in, distortions of memory, things that other people have said about him, other pictures they have painted.

But I never can climb the Alhambra hill or pass the old Washington Irving Hotel (now battered and closed) without hearing that warm voice, seeing that totally engaging smile, and the shape of those brown hands on the rough-toned upright piano. Reading his later poetry in Spanish is at times an effort, for the Federico who wrote much of it has become a stranger. Only in some of it will the voice sound, only in *Poet in New York* will the hidden terror, blanketed so successfully at the time, come forth and the magic charm of remembered personality take hold to banish the shadows.

That his work continues to outlive him would be his fondest epitaph.

Mildred Adams
New York 1977

GARCÍA LORCA:
Playwright and Poet

1

CHAPTER

"Running Wild"

FEDERICO GARCÍA LORCA, POET, DRAMATIST and without intention a political martyr, was neither a gypsy nor a Communist. He began life as the second son of a farm owner in greenest Andalusia. His father was a successful agriculturalist in the emerald valley that stretches east from the gaunt Granada hills. Described as "a bull of a man," Don Federico García Rodríguez's proportions were ample, his square face and hands were burned by the sun to the true Arab brown. A fierce black mustache, and a heavy gold watch chain stretched across his front, both of which he cherished, distinguished him from his fellow farmers. He looked exactly what he was—a solid rural citizen with a comfortable income and a good reputation for competence with land and horses. He did not look like a man to whom poetry would mean very much.

Federico's mother had a similar Andalusian ancestry, but a very different temperament. Admired as a schoolteacher and a musician (she brought a piano as part of her marriage portion) Doña Vicenta Lorca Romero* was quiet and discreet, short of body and softly curved, an amiable and affectionate woman with a gentle and almost

*Spanish usage combines the names of father and mother, putting the mother's name last. It is not without significance that Federico called himself familiarly Lorca, rather than García.

childish voice. She came to the García house in Fuente Vaqueros as a second wife. Her well-to-do predecessor had died childless. Doña Vicenta bore baby Federico in the same bed.

The family house is two stories high, made of sun-dried brick plastered white, set in a walled garden where children could safely play. The town around it is flat, dusty, made mostly of low white buildings that present a solid wall to the passerby and make a main street dazzling under the sun. Two churches point cross-topped steeples toward the sky. Traffic coming in from the highway on the north finds the town a dead end, and few casual travellers have reason to brave the rutted road. An oxcart, a swarm of bicycles pedalling home from the sugar factory on the north, a herd of sheep nodding along in a cloud of dust, and little more, except at nightfall when the farmers, the carts and the animals come back from the fields. This is Fuente Vaqueros as the sign points to it today—it did not look different in 1898.

In the beginning young Federico García Lorca was sturdy enough. But at two months a strange fever struck and endangered his life. Whatever its name, it reduced him to listless frailty, making him slow to walk, slow to talk, able to murmur only the music of folk tunes sung to him by his mother and his nurse. He did not say words until he was three, did not walk about until he was four, and then with a haunting limp that continued to show fatigue.

His mother adored him the more for his frailty, but his father could not happily accept weakness. He wanted a son who could run, play and ride farm horses like the other village boys. At two years of age he had Federico photographed on a hobbyhorse with four white feet and a decorated hide, a horse shaped like the massive creatures that Velasquez used to paint for armored kings to ride on;

this the boy beat violently because it would not move forward like the horse his father rode. At six Federico was photographed again, this time unsmiling, in shoes that laced above the ankles, knickers that came below the knees, a jacket with a truncated sailor collar and a flowing black tie; posed in front of painted scenery, he was holding carefully to a carved wooden screen.

His earliest education began at home. His mother taught the frail boy his letters and introduced him to written music (folk songs filled the house for most of the day); then she sent him to the village school where she herself had taught. Later he followed his schoolteacher to a grammar school in Almería, on the coast, seventy-five miles away. First he was homesick, the other boys teased him; he missed above all the affectionate atmosphere of warm understanding which surrounded him at home. This was, he said later, "the unhappiest time of my life." Finally he fell ill, and his face swelled until, as he told a friend, he looked like the royal Moorish fat man. Whether it was mumps, a bad tooth, or some obscure psychosomatic ailment, he was sick enough so that his father came to take him home. He was not sent away again.

If school was troublesome, play presented no problems. Most of the time Federico, endlessly inventive, amused himself, his new brother and two sisters as they came along, his nurse and his mother. Sometimes a puppet show came to the village and then he made his own puppet theater. Always there flourished the stories that had accumulated in the minds of elders. Verbally embroidered, richly dramatic, these were passed on to children as they came, with no hampering fear that young lives might be blasted by a touch of terror. Little Red Riding Hood was not rewritten to spare the feelings of Spanish children; at the end the wolf did eat her up. And Federico, on whom childhood left impressions that he was never to forget, once began a lecture on lullabies by saying, "I wanted to go down to the rushes by the river's edge. Underneath the yellow tiles. To the end of the town, where the tiger eats little boys."

The dreams that colored his childhood held sharper images than the admonishing threats of imaginary tigers. These included a haunting memory of the brother named Luís, born when he was very young, who died almost at once but was always alive for Federico.

Then his uncle told a tale of two bandits who appeared in the barn one night, seeking shelter and a cup of water, "things that are denied to no one." The family took pity on them. Field straw in the loft gave an ample bed; bandits and tired farm hands slept. At midnight they were awakened by a heavy tread and a shout, "Make way for the Civil Guard!" Lanterns shone on three-cornered patent leather hats and rifle barrels. They also lit the ashen face of one of the bandits, dead in the night of an unconfessed wound, unmoving in the straw. The other blinked in the sudden light but said nothing. Finally, the guards marched him away.

"And you," they said to Federico's uncle and the farm hands, "shut your mouths and tell no one what you saw."

"What did they do to the man?" asked young Federico at this point.

"We heard a shot, a cry, then another shot and nothing more," replied his father.

"They killed him!" said the boy, big-eyed. "They killed him." Doña Vicenta shook her head protesting, "Why do you tell such things to a child?"

Don Federico shrugged his heavy shoulders. "He will have to know them some day."

In time, the folk tales of the village were supplemented for the Lorca children by the plays that Federico began constructing for his own amusement. The gift of a toy theater helped. He had a faithful audience at hand in his brother Francisco and his sisters Concha and Isabel, a visiting cousin or two, at times his mother or the peasant maids. Dolores, his brother's nurse—whom he used later as model for the servant in *Blood Wedding (Bodas de Sangre)* and in *Doña Rosita*—showed herself the ideal spectator, for she could be depended on at indicated moments to shout with laughter or to weep torrents of tears.

Even in those early days the theater was to him a passionate and absorbing game in which he performed as playwright, actor, director. One moment he was draping the peasant maids in long linen towels and curtains to make them look like Moorish captives, the next he himself was playing the characters he had outlined—a servant in a wealthy family, an old woman visiting the Mother Superior in a convent, a thick-tongued peasant from a nearby village. His imagination, his gusto, his dramatist's power of persuading his audience to respond as he desired came early into practice.

Meanwhile he was absorbing into his poet's mind and his dramatist's imagination details of the way the *vega* looked and the turns of picturesque peasant speech in which its life and its people were discussed. Andalusia is a land of exaggerated and colorful language, poured out as a necessary expression of living, but having relatively little modern literary recognition. What Federico did again and again was to take the country figures of speech and incorporate them into the highly allusive poetic shorthand which distinguished his later verse.

Much later he said of himself that "being a child, I lived in a full atmosphere of nature. Like all children, I judged the personality of each thing, each object, each piece of furniture, each tree, each stone. I talked with them and I loved them. In the patio of our house grew black poplars. One afternoon it occurred to me that the poplars were singing. The wind, moving through their branches, produced a variety of tones which seemed to me music. And I spent hours accompanying with my voice the song of the poplars. Another day I was astonished to hear an old black poplar pronounce my name, 'Fe-de-ri-co' by rubbing one branch against another." Or so his ego told him.

With all this, his was a guarded childhood in the sense that his parents were responsible people who believed in a certain amount of order and did not let their children run wild. His farmer father was quick-tempered, hard riding, all for discipline. His mother was more amenable, but firm with her children. Federico's phrase about his parents is that they "withdrew from the vulgar shout."

In his first published book of poems he speaks of himself as "running naked" in his "impassioned infancy" across meadows with mountains in the background, but if he ever escaped from the house to the street with no clothes on, even at the age of two or three, it was behind his mother's back and against her will. A friend's tale of Doña Vicenta standing just so much noise from singing games in the great inner yard where the children played, and then calling down, "Children, children, less of that scandalous racket! What will the neighbors say?" comes closer to the observed truth.

In later years Federico told a reporter that "my earliest memories have the flavor of the earth. The country has done great things in my life. The earth, insects, the animals, the country people have ideas that come to very few. I now seize them with the same spirit as in my childhood . . .

"I was a curious child [he was then 8] and I followed

the vigorous plowing of my father's land all across the countryside. I liked to see the enormous steel blades open a gash in the earth, a gash from which roots sprang in place of blood. Once the plow stopped. Something resisted it. A second later the brilliant steel blade threw up out of the earth a bit of Roman mosaic. It held an inscription which I no longer remember, but the names of the shepherds Daphnis and Chloe have stayed in my mind. They too have a flavor of earth and love."

Three other prime elements of the *vega* also stayed with him and were fashioned into literary fame. One was the *duende,* another the local Punch and Judy shows of which the Spanish hero-villain is Don Cristóbal. A third was the Civil Guard. The *duende,* as Lorca described it later, is "the hidden spirit of our Spain of sorrows." It is one of the roots of the gypsy soul. "In all Andalusia . . . people talk constantly of the *duende,* and when it manifests itself they give it instant recognition." One of the great gypsy singers said to a younger aspirant, "You have the voice, you have the style, but you will never triumph because you have no *duende.*" And another, hearing Brailowsky play Bach, exclaimed, "Olé! That one has *duende!*"

To be recognized as having *duende* was Lorca's own ideal, and this gift, more than any other single factor, is perhaps the deepest secret of his continuing personal success. People who cannot read the language in which he wrote, who have never been to Spain, who have no basis for understanding the peculiarly local conditions and allusions which are so basic in his work—these people he reached by the force of this *duende* that stretches across all barriers to the heart and the imagination.

As for the effect of Don Cristóbal, Federico made him into a play, two plays. The Spanish Punch and Judy show (called *Títeres*), like the French Guignol, is a universal framework for human comment, a puppet play in which the characters are fixed and known, but the details may vary from place to place.

These marionette plays, far from being exercises in style, or miniature farces meant for children, are true theater and true Lorca. *The Puppets of Cachiporra (Los Títeres de Cachiporra), The Puppet Play of Don Cristóbal (Retablillo de Don Cristóbal),* have so much movement, so much verbal flavor, such sharp human suggestibility that they become not doll play but high comedy. One version was made to be played for soldiers in the Spanish Civil War. They are small, shrewd cousins of Lorca's inimitable *The Shoemaker's Prodigious Wife (Zapatera Prodigiosa)* and quite as enticing to a critic's notice.

As for the third element of the *vega* that made a lasting imprint on the young man's mind, the Civil Guard, this took on the very color of evil itself, so much so that their patent leather hats became the symbol of arrogant and heartless power. Among his gypsy ballads he wrote one that made the Guard infamous wherever Lorca's poetry is read. In Rolfe Humphries' translation it begins warningly:

Black are the black-shod horses.
Stains of ink and of beeswax
Gleam on the capes of the men.
Their deadly faces are leaden,
Therefore they never weep:
Hearts of patent leather
They come along the road.
Twisted, crooked, nocturnal
They sow in the places they haunt
Sombre elastic silence,
Fears that trickle like sand. . . .

And at the end, they wreck the town, while

Rosa de los Camborios
Sobs on the step of her door
With both breasts cut away
And placed on a serving tray.

The *vega*'s imprint was not a light one.

2

CHAPTER

Tortillas Made of Twilight

THE ELEVEN YEARS THAT FEDERICO spent on the *vega* were far from stationary. As his father prospered and bought new farms, he moved his family from one polysyllabic village to another. His son's poems record their names—Fuente Vaqueros and Valderrubio, the Vega de Zujaira, Lanjarón and San Vicente, all of them farm villages on the plain, all of them within reach of the Moorish vestiges of Granada, all of them possessed of rural treasures that enchanted Federico at whatever age. The boy's travels within and among them lengthened as he grew. In and out of the house and the gardens where he delighted to watch lizards and insects while he was little, up and down the green and watery *vega* when he could run farther, off to Almería to school and to Malaga for the beach and the salt water; then in 1909, when he was eleven, came the portentous family decision that they would move to Granada in order to get more advanced schooling for him, his sisters, and his younger brother.

In many ways, this was a major decision, and it involved major changes. Not only did the García Lorcas leave all the familiar sights and sounds of country life, the familiar friends, the freedom of movement, but the very process of moving was both gigantic and revolutionary.

For weeks the peasant maids were busy packing linen and furniture, clothes and silver and china; on a day in September they piled the family possessions into great horse-drawn farm wagons which took them across the *vega* to the high road, then on, under the dusty plane trees, to the new town house in a town street in Granada. There, life would be very different for all of them.

Federico's health was very much more dependable than it had been in earlier years, but that infant illness had left him a sensitivity to his own feeling of well or ill that he never lost. His dependence on his mother and her standards, with the conflicts—open or repressed—that developed in his later years, had their origin in that illness. So did the repeated battles between the child and his father, which became more marked in his adolescence, have their roots in that frail childhood, when tears came too easily as did anger. Don Federico was not a father to suffer weakness happily.

Yet there is every reason to believe that he did the best he could for his children and their futures. Hard as the move away from his farms must have been for him, the decision, once made, was carried into action, and he set himself to the new demands of the new town surroundings. He had been born in Granada, but time had changed what he remembered.

For the children, the move was infinitely exciting at first, but it did not always continue to be completely satisfactory. They missed their friends, and it was not always easy to make approved new ones. Their playground on the *vega* had been the family garden, then the succession of towns and villages, then the whole width and length of the green *vega.* Now it narrowed in physical proportions, while it widened in mental prospects. They were to play in the familiar "Paradise closed to many, garden opened to a few" which was the way that the 17th century poet,

Soto de Rojas, described all Granada. Federico himself revived that description three hundred years later.

The town was still a garden, but very different from the one Federico had known as a child. Not so flat as the *vega,* nor so big, nor so completely filled with sunshine. A patio garden surrounded with walls entered through grilled doors, or one of those delicious *carmens* of Granada which boast not only a fountain and a wall but also an irrigating tank, a small orchard and a kitchen garden, as well as more formal spaces for walks and flowers. What lay inside those gardens he made the subject as well as the setting for his poems—the lizards, the fountains, the roses and cypresses, the waxen flowers with a heavy fragrance which the Spaniards call *nard,* the spice carnations, the palm trees, and everywhere the green that became his symbol and signword—"Green wind, green branches. Green, how I love you, green."

The house was more formal than the village ones had been. A photograph of one Granada interior, reproduced in Angel del Río's affectionate book on Lorca, shows the poet and his sister Concha studying at a long table with flowers beside them, a wide window in the background, family portraits on the wall above a row of high-backed chairs. Another day the two were photographed sitting self-consciously in a favorite "cosy corner" furnished with wicker chairs, heavily striped wallpaper, a two-handled copper jar loaded with flowers, and above their heads a plate rail lined with Spanish-Moorish lustreware. It was the setting for a very comfortable and proper middle-class family.

There would be no more "running wild across the *vega,*" in fact or in imagination. Instead, the country boy was now a city boy, with all the furnishings of propriety expected for a child of good family. He was entered in a preparatory school named the Sacred Heart of Jesus, where his father had ordained that he was to prepare for that vital document in Spanish education, the *bachillerato,* equivalent to a high school degree.

Despite its name, the Sacred Heart of Jesus was not a church school, but its teaching was in line with the strictest Catholic orthodoxy. Its director, Don Joaquín Alemán, was a first cousin of Doña Vicenta, its professors were neither young nor progressive. The teacher of geography, for one, was said to be "deaf as a mud wall, an intransigent religious devotee, and the victim of terrible toothaches." None of this could have contributed either to his patience or his understanding of his charges. The professor of literature went mad and read his own erotic verses to his students as commendable examples of poetic composition.

A third professor lives on in the third act of Federico's play *Doña Rosita the Spinster, or the Language of the Flowers (Doña Rosita La Soltera, o el Languaje de las Flores).* Described as "a noble type, with great dignity and an air of definite sadness," he moans, "I've just come from lecturing to my class in Precepts. A real hell! It was a wonderful lecture: 'Concept and Definition of Harmony' but the children weren't interested at all—and what children! For me, since they see I am disabled, they have a little respect. Now and then some pin or other in the chair, or a little paper doll on my back; but to my companions they do horrible things. They are the children of the rich and, since they pay, we can't punish them. This the director is always telling us. . . . Every day I enter the school trembling, waiting to see what they are going to do to me."

In such an atmosphere it is not surprising that young Federico studied very little and learned less. In October 1916, when he was eighteen years old, he was expected to move from the preparatory school to the General and Technical Institute of Granada, and toward that end he took his first serious examination. This he failed, but for unexplained reasons the Institute let him in. Influence was, and still is, powerful in Granada, and of that the García Lorca family had plenty.

Years later the poet told his critic friend, Giménez de Caballero, "I studied hard in the Sacred Heart of Jesus, I knew a great deal in those days. But in the Institute they failed me again and again. Later, in the University, I failed in literature, in precepts, in the history of the Spanish language, but I became enormously popular because of the nicknames I invented for my schoolmates."

Another friend cast a somewhat dubious eye on this summary, recalling both the poet's love of distortion and the critic's astigmatic wit. Angel del Río believed there were actually five failures—all in handwriting (alas for the non-conforming charm of that delicate and imperative Lorquian tracery!). A sixth would have resulted in the student's suspension, but as a superior intelligence was showing itself in other areas of study, his teachers decided to pass him, however outraged they might be by his unconventional penmanship.

His explorations into the family books and those in the libraries of new friends also form the subject of controversy. His friend Martínez Nadal credits him with having been a tireless reader of the classics, the romantics, and the contemporary Spanish writers—the so-called "generation of '98"—and claims that he also read in Spanish translation "the best of the French classics, especially the tragedies, and a vast repertoire of modern foreign literature." On the other hand, the late José Montesinos, brother of the charming youth whom Federico's sister Concha married, and until recently teaching at Berkeley, contradicts this flatly, calls it a legend, and says that "no one among contemporary poets read less." Angel del Río, weighing the evidence as displayed in Lorca's own writings, takes a middle ground. He credits the poet with having read Cervantes, and among French authors, Victor Hugo who was his father's favorite; in translation, Ibsen and Shakespeare "whose entire work he read when very young and continued to read all his life." Through friends, he knew something of Maeterlinck, Verlaine, the French Symbolists.

Of other Spaniards besides Cervantes, he devoured those poets who were "modern" while he was growing up —Angel Ganivet, his mother's delight, who committed suicide while a consul in Scandinavia, the brothers Machado, the Nicaraguan Rubén Dario whose sensuous vocabulary stimulated the so-called "modernist revolt" in Spanish poetry. Juan Ramón Jiménez and the prose poet Azorín he knew personally. The older Zorilla he openly admired, and the romantic Becquer, as well as the 16th century Góngora, to whom he paid warm tributes, including inspiration. Later, he added a familiarity with Jean Cocteau and with the American Walt Whitman, whom he celebrated in one of his most famous odes.

Some of this literature he may have acquired more by a process of absorption than by detailed reading. He had an extraordinary sensitivity to all that took place around him, and an amazing memory for the spoken word, which showed itself in his theatrical dialogue. In addition, what Lorca did not know he had the ability to invent, and frequently his invention coincided with the fact.

By nature he was a poet; he was also a musician of no mean ability. He had studied first with his mother; then with "an old music master, delicate and sad . . . Lorca learned to play Beethoven, the romantics—Mendelssohn, Schubert, Schumann, the Spaniard Albéniz—with a certain smooth and trembling touch that spoke of faded flowers." The "faded flowers" he got over; when he was sixteen he gave a concert in the echoing auditorium of the

Centro Artístico in Granada, and his playing of Beethoven sonatas so impressed the man who was then President of the Center that he took the promising youngster under his wing.

This bearded man with the kind eyes was Fernando de los Rios, then one of the few progressive professors in the University of Granada. Federico's music had won him a friend and advisor whose influence would affect his entire life. Federico made other friends, sometimes by chance, sometimes by direct and deliberate effort. José Mora Guarnido's description of his own meeting with the youth was typical of a certain young directness. He was a couple of years older than Federico, already acknowledged in Granada as a leader in literary matters, and well enough known so that the younger man yearned to meet him. Chance did not bring them together, but on the street one day, without introduction or apology, the eighteen-year-old stopped him, held out a hand, and said, "I am Federico García Lorca." He did it "without any timidity, with the emphasis of one who feels within himself the certainty of an outstanding destiny, and in the tone of one who knows that he is *somebody.*" Dressed in dark clothes, with a broad-brimmed hat so flexible that it moved in the wind "like a big butterfly's wing," he looked the part of a student belonging to a good family.

With the same direct approach, Federico asked at once about a paper that Mora Guarnido had written on the 16th century poet Góngora, and then about the deep rivalry that existed between two groups of young devotees of culture in the town. Walking on, apparently without a goal, but led by Federico, they reached his family's home. "Shall we go up?" asked the younger man. The older agreed. In a big and comfortable house the two made their way to a wide living room that imposed quiet by its "curtains and hangings, rugs and furniture without style, but harmonizing delicately into a gracious whole . . . a room which might well have been the scene of *Doña Rosita the Spinster,* with old pictures, family portraits, a great crystal lamp with a rosy silk shade, a piano between two balconies that gave on the street, and at each side of the piano a large easy chair and a music cabinet." So Mora Guarnido described the setting for this sudden new friendship.

The two talked long and eagerly of literary interests. The younger man played a Chopin nocturne as casually as if it were another form of speech. They talked again. At the end of the afternoon they had crossed the barrier between acquaintance and friendship. Federico had found another new ally.

The transition from country to city produced moments of nostalgia as well as new friends. At times Federico began to feel cramped in spirit as well as in body. In his "Ballad of the Little Square" ("Balada de la Placeta") he tells the children playing there that he was going "very far away, far beyond the mountains, far beyond the seas, close up to the stars." What he did was to make new friends, to read, to play, to range the Alhambra hill and the gypsy quarter on the other side of town—in short, to do almost anything but the studying that was expected of him when the family moved from the *vega* into the provincial capital. This course did not please his elders, especially it did not please the stern and downright father. The boy must get his *bachillerato* if he was to get on in the world—this was why the family had come to the city—and getting on was the elder Federico's chief aim in life. Yet his son would not study, he played tricks, he was the ring leader in all sorts of plots aimed to embarrass his professors who had the power to flunk him.

Nevertheless, the town of Granada was, even in those dull days, a place where influence could be exerted, and was. Somehow things were managed so that the *bachillerato* did come forth. Entrance to the University followed, but not with much more success on Federico's part. The father still wanted his eldest son to study law. The son had a vague interest in philosophy, a considerable interest in letters, but none at all in legal matters. So, after a great deal of family pressure and internal anguish, he was entered in all three.

Meeting anecdotes of the temperamental boy, in print or in conversation, one wonders why his practical father ever dreamed that the law could be the boy's lifetime occupation. It was, and still is, a traditional Spanish occupation for the middle class, entirely proper and polite. It would give this most impractical of sons a means of livelihood. Also Don Federico was of the school that believed the tree grows as the sapling is bent. If it ever occurred to him that this sapling would resist his most earnest efforts at bending, he did not admit it. He was not accustomed to being defied in the fields, the markets or the household. The father's effort at bending went on. So did the son's resistance.

In accounts of Lorca's higher education the customary uncertainty has left puzzles. One biographer says that in 1915 he did manage to pass the final examination for that *bachillerato,* which he had needed in order to enter the University where he had matriculated the year before. How this was managed, in view of his failures to pass examinations, is one of those Spanish mysteries. What happened after he got in is also a matter of vague anecdotes and conflicting memories. In the official biography written with family aid, José Luís Cano says, "If suspensions did not rain down on him, it was due to the kindness of certain of the professors, especially Don Fernando de los Rios" (who had discovered a musician, not a student) and three other professors who "showed benevolence toward the indolent boy who was already writing verses and who played the piano so well."

He had then three major interests: the first was

music; the second was poetry; the third was the gypsy quarter. Music, begun when he was a very small boy in Fuente Vaqueros, had, by the time he reached adolescence, become a matter of very considerable skill. He had lessons both in the piano and the guitar, and he played both instruments throughout his life. In Granada he had the great luck to make friends with the composer, Manuel de Falla, who taught him a great deal. Poetry in the formal sense he was just beginning; the earliest poem in his first book of poems is attributed to the year 1915.

The wild and romantic charm of Granada's gypsy quarter added a new dimension. Not that the gypsies as such were strange to him—gypsies he had met, with their picturesque garb and their unrestrained ways, on the *vega.* But their town center was the Albaicín hill, on the other side of Granada. Here they lived in caves or mud houses, here their charming children played, their beautiful daughters sang and danced, their old men told tales, and the Civil Guard came hunting implacably whenever there was a theft, a murder, a tragedy big or little.

Lorca's second interest, poetry, rapidly became his first. He never gave up music, but neither could he be said to have advanced much further in it as a creative artist. Rather, he made of it a useful tool, a handmaid. Poetry, on the contrary, spurred him and shaped him. By nature an intensely verbal person, growing up in a region that was mostly illiterate but highly articulate, he early learned by ear more easily and happily than by eye. His long reluctance to submit his poems to print shows how deeply he preferred to communicate by physical and personal means. He seemed to have antennae out in every direction to bring him the speech, the songs, the folk tales and the verbal traditions of those around him. At an early age he showed himself an incomparable mimic, and this skill he carried into his theater dialogue.

Granada provided the cultural paths and the people he needed. In spite of its barren commercial aspect, the town had a somewhat frail literary tradition which was never forgotten and which for generation after generation spurred the young. Soto de Rojas at the end of the 16th century, Zorilla in the 19th were the names that Granada cherished, but a new movement had begun with the generation of 1898; its most recent fruit was a still younger magazine called "Andalucía 1915." Plagiarist this may have been, copying the form of "España 1915" published in Madrid, and living no longer than a poppy blossom, but its two numbers "testified to a state of mind, a resolution to plan and to emphasize certain values which, although frustrated, could be considered characteristic of a generation with high aspirations and a restless conscience."

Federico was too young to have played a part in the production of "Andalucía 1915," or of "España 1915" which had set the pattern for it; he had begun his public career as a musician in the *Centro Artístico* of Granada, but he took pains to meet the youthful group that had declared war on the *Centro* and had produced "Andalucía 1915." This group continued to display its own wares and attitude in local newspapers. It was one of these articles, defending the difficult 16th century poet Góngora, which led to Federico's approach to Mora Guarnido who had written it, and in the latter's mind, at least, had provided the spark which would transform Lorca the musician into Lorca the poet.

This younger group had no such established meeting place as the older *Centro,* but it had found a home in one corner of the Café Alameda, and from that coined for itself the name *El Rinconcillo,* Little Corner. Here, and with some care not to disturb the more profitable older clients of the café, these young intellectuals met regularly to discuss books and book values, poets, essayists, novelists. They also considered painters and playwrights, the sad state of commercial Granada, the new music of Debussy and Ravel. As their fame grew they found themselves visited not only by the composer Manuel de Falla who had recently come to live in Granada and brought with him his friend, the Polish harpsichordist Wanda Landowska, but also by such foreign tourists as H. G. Wells and Rudyard Kipling, and the Japanese diplomat Nagaka Koichi. Here the young tried out their ideas, their literary discoveries, their phrases and their poetry on each other and on the famous. It was a type of mutual education that later made an American critic exclaim, "God, how these Spaniards can talk!"

For Federico, *El Rinconcillo* was at once a school. infinitely preferable to the University, and a stage. Here he made warm friends and had a sympathetic audience. Mora Guarnido believes that it was only with the encouragement of the group that he began to write poetry. Certainly this body of talented and ambitious youths supplied for the younger one the very savor of literary life for which he yearned. It measured him, it praised him, it made him appear worthy in his own eyes at a time when his father, still wanting him to be a lawyer, appeared most annoyed, most censorious, most irritating and irritated. Unbearable as this attitude was from Federico's point of view, to a solid Andalusian farmer a burgeoning poet in the family must have been worse than a case of colic in a favorite horse.

Yet there were compensations. Mora Guarnido supplies a pertinent anecdote. It was one of Don Federico's implacable orders that children must arrive on time at the family evening meal. His eldest son, with his habitual disregard of the clock, frequently came late. One night he arrived even later than usual. When he did come in, his annoyed father asked him if he thought the house was an inn, told him not to be late again, and announced, "Beginning tomorrow, anyone who does not arrive on time is not to sit at the table."

Federico, equally furious, retorted, "Then I will not sit down. I do not want to shut myself in the house at the hour of twilight!"

The table was silent. What would Federico the elder do? Before he had time to discharge another clap of thunder, the maid came in with an innocent question, "What kind of a tortilla would Master Federico like?"

It was the irritated father who answered furiously, "Make it of chrysanthemums, of violets, of twilight!"

Federico shouted with laughter, and the others, sensing the relief of tension, joined in. The victory went both to father and son. The next time Federico's seat was vacant at the appointed hour, his father pronounced what became a family joke, "The boy will be eating his tortilla made of twilight. May it do him good. We are going to eat ours made of ham!"

Bit by bit the boy was winning his independence. The arguments were frequent and did not always end with a jest. The father's desire that Federico junior become a lawyer, even though he might never practice, was firm. That he stay in the University and get his law degree was finally the only sacrifice that the older man demanded. Economically, Don Federico could well afford to support a writing son. But to the father's eyes, what a useless career! To live writing verses! In an effort to deter his son he kept repeating tales of poets who had gone abroad and died in exile.

Federico made his first public appearance as a writer not with verses but with a group of essays recording his impressions of Spain. He had taken two summer trips out of Andalusia with a group of friends led by a favorite professor, and out of these he garnered subjects. These young essays were derivative, not exciting, but sufficiently suggestive of new talent that a Granada publishing house could be persuaded to bring them out in 1918. But a book of that type, in that time, written by a writer barely beginning to be known, would not pay its way. Federico sought paternal help. His father consulted Fernando de los Rios and Manuel de Falla. One evening he met Mora Guarnido on his way to a meeting of *El Rinconcillo.* "As you know," he said abruptly, biting his customary Havana cigar, "I don't mind spending two or three thousand pesetas to give him the pleasure that he will get from this book. It would cost more if he were to ask for an automobile. But I don't want all the idiots of Granada to laugh at him." And then the key question, "Have you read the manuscript?"

Mora Guarnido replied that he had. Moreover, he considered it worth publishing, and he himself—if he had a book of that quality—would want it published. As for laughter, if the boys in *El Centro* wanted to make a joke or two, let them. Don Federico listened carefully. The book was published.

Members of *El Rinconcillo* promptly took part of the glory to themselves. They also shared in Federico's disgrace when his lack of application to studies was followed by the inevitable failures in his university courses. He would not, he could not apply himself to the dry areas of law, logic and allied subjects. The whole family suffered with him, as well as his friends. Failure in May examinations meant that the student had to go through his assignments during the summer in order to try exams again in September. This meant that the family had to stay in Granada province during the hot months. They could not go out to enjoy sea breezes in Malaga but had to be content with the June harvest time in the *vega.* Then back to the city heat in Granada.

Blame fell not only on Federico but also on his *El*

Rinconcillo friends. Even patient Doña Vicenta complained. "Why didn't you study, and make him study?" she asked. Family and friends collectively and separately did their best. His fellow students entered into discreet conspiracies to get him through. They wrote his papers for him; they begged for lenience from his professors; and some of the latter, recognizing the exceptional quality of the errant boy who could not, would not be confined to the classroom's usual ways, were so gentle in their markings as to give reason for Don Federico to smile again.

Whether Federico junior ever got his full degree or not is one of those uncertainties that characterize his life. Cano, the biographer that the much-photographed family helped, says that he never did get his degree in philosophy and letters, though the law degree came to him in 1923. Needless to say, he never exercised one iota of the legal license it granted him.

In 1919 Federico was twenty-one years old, still financially dependent on his father, but matured to the point where older, better educated men of wide literary experience set themselves to watch the development of his talents. Except for its beauty of landscape and architecture, he had outgrown Granada. Except that he continued to love it as part of his bone and blood, he had outgrown Andalusia. The wider life of the capital called him. Fernando de los Rios persuaded his father that the talented young man should continue his education in Madrid, where he could live and learn in the free atmosphere of the *Residencia de Estudiantes.*

3

CHAPTER

First Play on Stage

FEDERICO'S VENTURE INTO MADRID MARKED an entirely new life and a new attitude toward living. He had been a romantic provincial; now, although romantic tendencies still characterized his writing, he began to fancy himself a sophisticated resident of Madrid.

He had made his appearance in Madrid with the typical wardrobe of a prosperous boy from the provinces who intended to make his way at court; he brought numerous new suits, including the inevitable black one, at least one pair of patent leather shoes in addition to ordinary ones, and an ample supply of white shirts with starched piqué fronts. He also had his intellectual suitings—a list of the Granada friends who had preceded him, including Manuel Montesinos who sought, and later won, the hand of his sister Concha; the author Melchor Fernández Almagro and the Granadan guitarist Angel Barrios—along with a bundle of letters introducing him to others already famous in the literary circles of Madrid.

More important in terms of his literary status were copies of his first book, that *Impressions and Landscapes (Impresiones y Paisajes)* for which his father had paid publishing costs after hearing from Mora Guarnido that it was well worth printing. Of this collection of schoolboy travel sketches, he was at first proud, then apologetic. In Granada he had thought that the book would serve as his passport to the literary world, a proof that he had already passed from being merely an aspiring provincial from Granada, a testimonial to his wider view of all Spain. But once in Madrid, he very quickly changed his mind.

Few people have read that collection of travel essays, nor can they read much of it in Federico's *Complete Works (Obras Completas).* When the critic Guillermo de Torre came to edit the first edition of those *Works* he omitted the early essays, judging them "tender," and sure that "Neither would the author have included them." On the other hand Professor Angel del Río of Columbia wrote about this young effort with surprising enthusiasm. "I confess without a blush," said he, "that I always had a certain weakness for this book. Prose of an almost 'cursi' romanticism, very 1898, now all out-dated, yet one could see in it, ingenuous and rough, some of the outstanding aspects of García Lorca's later work. Romanticism, penetration into the traditions of the people, plasticity, color, dramatism, musical feeling. There was the constant pressure of passion, of night, of blood, an impressive obsession with death, an intuitive and vital feeling for the world and for poetry. All this, which is in the great themes of romantic literature . . . an eternal romanticism which is a constant dimension of the human soul and art."

But in 1918 Federico was already beginning to outgrow his first book, and he knew it. He had also brought with him a more mature essay praising the old Granada poet Zorilla, but the most important focus of his present hopes was a sheaf of poems which he had read to his friends and kept on reading, poems which were not yet published.

His friend, Professor Fernando de los Rios, who had persuaded the poet's father to let him leave home for the city, had assumed that the young Lorca could enter at once into the *Residencia de Estudiantes,* but for various reasons this was not possible. So he went first to a pension on the second floor of Calle San Marcos 36, where his Granada friend José Mora Guarnido, now a student at the University of Madrid, had already found lodgings. For the first months the young men shared a room without too much sense of crowding, for University studies took Mora Guarnido out early, and sent him to bed before Federico. The arrangement, by description, satisfied the anxious heart of the poet's mother, although she might have been less content had she known that a beautiful young dancer named Argentinita was living in the same house.

The first goal of his hopes in Madrid, the *Residencia,* was a well known student center whose hospitality the young had coveted for a decade. Its inspiration came from the theories of a German educator named Krause; its ideals and practices were those of an ample, sincere and disinterested European culture, overlaid with tutorial techniques worked out in English universities. The *Residencia* was primarily a place for students to live while studying, and with considerable freedom to follow their own ambitions. They might pursue courses at the University of Madrid, which then had no dormitories of its own, or study art at the Prado Museum, or work for literary degrees in the National Library, or pursue lectures or scientific investigations within the *Residencia.* Music and art were encouraged. A French observer described the institution as "a citadel of Spanish humanism . . . an Oxford in Madrid."

Physical resources were as attractive as the institution's intellectual claims. Built high on a hill overlooking Madrid, it was, according to the writer Moreno Villa who lived there for years, a glorious retreat from "all those material complications that slow one down. A motherly fairy saw that everything was as it should be. And all the hours of the day were free for writing, for painting, for studying, for talking with friends. One paid a single monthly check for one's keep, and that was all." In Federico's case it was his father who paid the check.

This combination of intellectual stimulus and physical comfort, with a blessed freedom from personal discipline, delighted the young poet. The *Residencia* became for a decade his second home, full of lively potential friends and providing a grand piano to which he always had access for his own purposes, whether he was playing for himself or for the listeners who gathered as to a magnet.

The precise date when Federico moved from his lodgings with Mora Guarnido to this cultural paradise is hidden in the *Residencia* files of half a century ago. Dates on his poems, always suspect, indicate that he was back home in Granada during November and December 1918, and also during the spring of 1919. He oscillated between the family homes in Granada province, and his mental and cultural home in the *Residencia.* Despite his ambition, his rebellions, his elegant arrival in Madrid, he was not yet fully weaned.

Indeed that process was long and painful. He had come a long way since his ill and fragile boyhood, but he was still his mother's darling, and her fears for his safety, physical and moral, were all too well-founded. If there was one thing that Federico could not do well, it was to take care of himself—not at two months, not at four years, nor at ten years when the family moved to Granada, not at twenty-one when he went to Madrid. The amount of assistance, sometimes anxious, sometimes amused, which he needed in order to get through his short life was hardly to be believed. That he found it was a testimony to his charm and to the radiating sense of being a rare and valuable character whom many kinds of people would gladly help.

The years from 1919 (when he apparently entered the

Residencia) to 1929 (when he left Madrid for New York) fall easily into two five-year sectors—the period before 1924 when he met Salvador Dalí and the puzzling rush of surrealism, and the further years between 1924 and 1929 when the speed of life and the strength of Federico's energy both picked up. If he was in many ways a late starter, after he got started he went fast. His first play was produced in 1920; his first book of poems came out in 1921. Then came a period of living back and forth between Granada and the capital, collaborating with Falla in the great Granada song festivals, and taking his place among the best of Spain's poets at the Góngora festival in Seville. It was 1924 before he finished another book of poems for publication.

In Granada it was first his music that had attracted people to him, and at the *Residencia* it was also this that acted as a prelude to his Madrid career. His ability to make the friends he wanted had been demonstrated in Granada with Mora Guarnido and the members of *El Rinconcillo.* It did not fail him in the larger and more diverse world of the Madrid student center. "Yet," says the older observer, Moreno Villa, discreetly, "not all the students loved Federico. Some of them sensed his defect and kept their distance." He does not explain what he meant by "defect." But he adds that when the poet opened the grand piano and began to sing, even the suspicious and the skeptical yielded to his skill and his charm. Federico played well in those days, with a repertoire of classics, folk songs and current music which is described as extensive. "He had been brought up beside Falla's piano, had followed his work and shared in his ideas. With Falla he learned to listen to the classic and to the popular, and he came to choose the best of the peoples' music."

Also in his music he had the great advantage of confidence—he always sat down at the piano as a master, and he never disappointed his audience. The fascination produced in his hearers came in part from his happy gift of combining "the cultural and the popular, the infantile and fresh with the reflective and the strict interpretation. This is very Andalusian," comments Moreno Villa again, "and can be seen in the bull fighter, the singer and the dancer. They alternate between dynamic frenzy and the sacred, between enormous joy and the sob."

When someone, after hearing him play Chopin, Mozart, Ravel or Falla, would ask him to play some of the 18th and 19th century peasant music that he was collecting, a transfiguration would appear in both artist and audience. Federico's eyes came off the keys, his face lifted, his look broadened, and he began to sing with a delighted smile the folk songs that he later arranged for Argentinita and put on records. His voice was warm, husky, untrained, by no means good. But neither, in professional terms, were the voices of the great folk singers among the gypsies. In the first place they must have the *duende,* that mysterious presence akin to modern "soul." Then they learned from their forebears not only the various types and kinds of folk songs, but also the inflections, the modulations, the combination of light and dark, "enormous joy and the sob" which each folk singer in his separate way created for himself.

Much of this Federico had heard in the gypsy quarter of Andalusia, and he had heard Falla analyze and evaluate it. The young musician could not attempt the great expertise that *cante jondo*—the peculiar native "deep song"—demanded, but he did sing the simpler types, and sang them with such verve, such charm and gaiety, such somber feeling that critics placed him within the great order of minstrels. If his technique was imperfect, his *duende* was a born gift.

His first professional move from music and poetry to

theater came very early in his Madrid adventures. His quick skill in making friends at the *Residencia* and their enthusiastic delight in his ways had brought him naturally in touch with playwrights as well as poets and singers. Among the former was Don Gregorio Martínez Sierra, an older playwright and director, internationally successful. Among his well known plays was *Cradle Song (Canción de Cuna)* which Nance O'Neill made famous on Broadway in the 1920s. In Madrid he was director of the *Teatro Eslava* and constantly on the lookout for new talent. Thanks to the Catalan poet Eduardo Marquina, who later introduced Dalí to the *Residencia,* Don Gregorio came early under the spell of the young musician-poet. Hearing Federico recite a sympathetic group of poems about lizards, butterflies, cockroaches and small forms of life (the first of these was his "Encounter of an Adventurous Snail"), the impresario urged him to make a play out of them.

What young man taking his first steps in the artistic world of Madrid could refuse such a chance? Certainly not Lorca, who had amused himself with theater since his childhood on the *vega* when he dressed the family servants up in sheets to make Moorish captives out of them. The play he wrote out of his poems was given the title *El Maleficio de la Mariposa,* roughly translatable as *The Butterfly's Evil Spell.* His Granadan friend Mora Guarnido remembers that the title was not the author's, but was decreed by the producer who was going to present the play. He also remembers considerable doubt on the part of Federico and his friends that the play would succeed; some of them urged that it be withdrawn before production, on the grounds that it was much too difficult to transfer those evocative and imaginative bits of poetry, delicious when recited by the poet, to the more material and problematical surroundings of the theater. His less tactful friends implored him to tear it up. Federico himself is said to have written a letter to Don Gregorio offering to pay the expenses of preparation if he would withdraw the play.

The producer, however, continued firmly confident. There is no record of his reasons for undertaking so strange an adventure and one so unlike his own solid and dependably successful plays, but he alone continued to have faith in the venture. A combination of poetry, music and dance, it was not easy to mount or to produce. A few alterations were made in text and action to bring the play more closely into line with known prejudices of the Madrid public: changes were made in the scenery; costumes then thought daring were toned down. But nothing could alter the fact that Madrid playgoers, traditionally skeptical and unimaginative, were being asked to contemplate a drama in which actors and actresses would play the roles of insects.

The Butterfly's Evil Spell opened on March 22, 1920, in the *Teatro Eslava* of Madrid under the direction of Don Gregorio. It was to be played by a first-class company headed by Catalina Barcena, who was cast as the lady cockroach, and the dancer Argentinita as the fated Butterfly. She herself had arranged the dances.

The house was full, curious, but not friendly. From the moment the curtain rose it became clear that, when dressed as insects, even the best of casts was only funny. More laughter came than applause, more talking than listening or looking. Argentinita, clad in a transparent costume as the Butterfly, got whistles of approval, but even her own dance was badly conceived and lame. Typically, the audience split into those who were friends of Federico and those who were not. With Spanish fervor, they shouted at each other and at the actors until few scenes could be heard except in bits and pieces. The play went on to its end, but it was not repeated. Federico's friends began to refer to it as "Don Gregorio's Evil Spell."

The blow dealt by such a reaction to the poet's first play must have been a heavy one, but the young playwright summoned courage enough to attend the post-performance party, which, planned as a homage, turned into a wake. The repeated theme was the wonder that so experienced a play maker and play producer as Don Gregorio Martínez had failed to see the fatal weakness in this symbolic and fragile bit of poetry, which should never have been turned into solid theatrical fact. Federico's friends toasted "Don Gregorio's Evil Spell," in place of the Butterfly's.

The producer undoubtedly lost heavily in cash, if not in reputation. Yet the fact remains that for whatever reason, he did give the young poet the greatest gift in his power—a first night in a famous Madrid theater. A failure the ill-begotten play surely was, but that first starred night remains on Federico's record. In March 1920, when he was only twenty-two years old, he saw his first play produced on the Madrid equivalent of Broadway.

It was seven years before a second play appeared. His new historical drama, *Mariana Pineda,* was far enough along in 1925 so that it could be read to friends, but it was not presented on stage until June 1927. Again he had a famous actress, Margarita Xirgu, in the leading role, and this time the play won praise, but the opening was in Barcelona, not Madrid.

If his first appearance in the theater was a disaster, dropping him momentarily from his high position as a wonder child, his first formal appearance as a poet was a triumph. From the earliest days of his adolescence Federico had written poems, had read them to friends, but had very rarely seen them published. He had arrived in Madrid with a sheaf of poems in his pocket, but the early failure of his first play had deprived him of the courage to face the world with their publication. It took the active and forceful encouragement of a publishing friend to make him change his mind. Gabriel Maroto, a contemporary and admirer who had a small publishing firm of his own, had heard Federico read his poems more than once. Convinced of their excellence, he tried again and again to persuade their author to let him put them into a book. Finally, after months of unaccustomed begging, he took the manuscript (dog-eared by this time) away from the poet by force, wrote his own introduction of this new poet to the Madrid public, and put the poems into print. The book had no title but the simple *Book of Poems (Libro de Poemas).*

Federico himself came out of his own timidity far enough to provide a wistful preface which shows how badly he had been hurt by the failure of his play and how much he dreaded further public scorn. He had long had the habit of testing his poems by reading them to friends and getting immediate favorable response, but the public was another kind of monster. Desperately, he felt the need to placate its not impossible scorn for this work too. So he told it in his foreword, "In this book, all youthful ardor, and torture, and ambition beyond measure, I offer the precise image of my days of youth and adolescence—those days which link my recent infancy to this very moment—It would be fatal to despise this work which is so closely linked to my own life. . . . Over and above its faults, its certain limitations, this book has the virtue, among many others, of reminding me at every step of my passionate childhood, running naked across the *vega,* with the mountains tall in the background." At least its author would like it.

The poems are clearly the young work of a poet with great promise. Imagination, emotion, a vivid sense of observation, a fine feeling for words and rhythm take them out of the amateur class. The first one recounts those "Encounters of an Adventurous Snail" ("Encuentros de un caracol aventurero") which led to that first ill-fated theatrical attempt. As a poem it is as delightful as it was inadequate as the theme of a play. There is also the salute to an old lizard, "with the green frock-coat of a devil's abbé, his correct expression, and his starched collar; he has the very sad air of a dignified old professor." Sixty-eight poems—about Granada, the *vega,* young love, and a moving elegy to the Castilian princess Juana the Mad whose bones lie with those of her careless husband in the cathedral of Granada—a good harvest for the first formal appearance of a young poet of twenty-three, and certainly worth printing.

Coming out on June 15, 1921, the book created at first no great stir except among its author's loyal friends. Then, a month and a half later, *El Sol* of Madrid, the capital's most prestige-bestowing newspaper, printed an enthusiastic and discerning review by Adolfo Salazar, music critic, who hailed its author with the affirmative headline, "A New Poet." Soon afterward Federico was recognized by one of Spain's most notable poets of an older generation, Juan Ramón Jiménez, who invited the younger man to contribute to his new magazine, *Indice.* Two succeeding numbers of the fledgling review carried Lorca poems, and in Spanish terms a new poetic reputation was established. However much Federico García Lorca, playwright, had suffered from premature exposure of his first play, Federico García Lorca, poet, was clearly on his way.

The next few years showed him rising to become a star in a period of literary renaissance such as Spain had not known since 1898. That was the year of her military and naval disasters, and also the year of literary triumphs that still define her position in the artistic world. Now a whole crop of new poets was springing up to offer Federico comradeship and competition. Rafael Albertí in Malaga, José Bergamín in Madrid, Jorge Guillén from Seville, Pedro Salinas in Castile, Gerardo Diego, and half a dozen others—their names now speak the loneliness of exile, and those who still live are scattered from Vermont to Buenos Aires, but in the 1920s they were all young, all talented, and the new pride of Spain. Still too uncertain of reception in established journals, those who now are classed as the "generation of 1936" then set up little magazines of their own, short-lived, but offering places where the young could be read.

It was in this warm, friendly and competitive atmosphere that Federico was earning his laurels as a poet and learning his trade as a professional dramatist. The two skills developed not separately and successively, as is sometimes believed, but hand in hand. Thus in 1922 Lorca went down to Granada to work with Maestro Falla on the latter's great festival of *cante jondo* (deep song) and in the same year he wrote a group of gypsy songs which, although not published until 1931 (his disinclination to publish presented a continuing problem to his admirers), bore the unmistakable mark of the festival. So does his still popular book, *Gypsy Ballads (Romancero Gitano),* written after the gypsy songs but published earlier.

The festival of *cante jondo* was a joint production of Federico and his friend and teacher, Manuel de Falla. The composer, recognizing that the traditional songs of Andalusia were being sung by imitators in a degraded form, planned a singing competition in Granada to show what was the true form and style of this ancient art. His great prestige among European musicians spread the news of this abroad, and the project gained the encouragement of poets, artists, and writers in France, England, and Germany. At the same time, word went out among the peasants and the gypsies of all Andalusia that a *cante jondo* competition for singers would be held in the *Patio de los Aljibes* of the Alhambra on the night of the full moon in June. Tryouts would be planned ahead of time, and only the best singers would be chosen to appear before the public. Expenses of all who entered would be paid, and on the great night there would be substantial cash prizes awarded to the winners. Picasso, already famous, would come down from Paris to make a suitable backdrop to hang in the beautiful old Moorish patio.

Federico, with Falla's encouragement, prepared an introductory lecture to explain the festival to its own people of Granada. The subject of the exercise, he said, is "a very rare example of primitive song, the oldest in all Europe, where examples of this historic ruin, the lyric fragments eaten by the sands of time, appear live as they were in the first morning of their creation."

To the gypsies, who are its usual and best singers, this "deep song" is a folk art, handed down in all its complexity from generation to generation. To foreigners it is as strange as it is remarkable. Strangers are most likely to hear it in Seville during Holy Week, but at times it can be heard in Madrid in what is called a *flamenco* show. Modern examples are likely to be commercial and weakly imitative, but usually they can at least hint of the real thing.

Lorca's essay attributed the development of "deep song" to a combination of elements, including the adoption by the Spanish Catholic Church of liturgical song, the Saracen invasion which brought to the peninsula for the third time a new torrent of Arabian blood, and the arrival of numerous bands of gypsies. "But let no one think that the gypsy 'sequiriya' and its variants are simply certain songs transplanted from the orient to the occident," Federico warned. "No. That is rather a coincidence of origin, which certainly was not revealed at a single specific moment, but which obeys the accumulation of historic and secular facts developed on our Iberian peninsula, and this is the reason why this song, although coinciding in its essential elements with a people geographically distant from ours, points up a character so much its own, which is so very national."

On the appointed night of the June full moon, Federico and his friends had a thousand details in hand. The audience in itself was remarkable. "The ladies of Granada had put on the silks and satins of a bygone generation, and wore them with inimitable grace. Marvelous flowered shawls, treasured heirlooms, had been taken out of their boxes to drape shoulders which even cold-blooded anthropologists admit to be modelled more beautifully than others." . . . So the Spanish expert, the late Professor J. B. Trend of Cambridge University, remembered it. "The voices in that velvet darkness, singing against the Picasso backdrop and with the dark gardens, crooked walls and scattered lights of the Albaicín [the gypsy quarter] rising behind it toward the sky seemed to a stranger as if they were trying to imitate the sounds of curious wood instruments. Yet the words were clearly audible, and were accompanied by the ghostly but intensely rhythmical twanging of a guitar, played by a master hand. . . . It was a moment of real musical emotion, the complete and perfect expression of the place and its tradition."

Six months later a special *Fiesta de los Reyes Magos* (Festival of the Magi) also added stage experience, had its influence and yielded its visible fruit. For it, Federico wrote a puppet drama (the beginning of a dramatic form seldom given its proper attention in his work) which bore the unhandy title *The Girl Who Waters the Basil and the Talkative Prince (La Niña que Riega la Albahaca y el*

Príncipe Preguntón). For this, designed primarily for children, Falla sat at the piano playing a musical commentary made out of fragments from Debussy, and the Spaniards Albéniz and Pedrell.

This puppet play has disappeared, but it was related to the composer's more serious work of the same period, and it forecast other and better known puppet plays by Lorca. At the same time the composer himself was writing the more finished and elaborate puppet opera, *Retablo de Maese Pedro,* with words from Cervantes. For the first production, given in a concert version in Seville during Holy Week, Federico designed the scenery. The play's formal debut took place in a beautifully fitted marionette theater set in the Parisian drawing room of the Princesse de Polignac who had commissioned it. Later, the artist Remy de Bufano put it on with his own puppets in New York.

Back in Madrid, Federico's progress continued to meet obstacles as well as successes. Not only did rivalries appear among younger and older poets which had to be combatted with new work, but the very currents of poetic expression around him were changing form and face. Romanticism was giving way to Dada and other surrealist strains, some of them brought in from France by way of surrealist writing, painting, speaking, some from renewed interest in the long-disregarded sixteenth-century Spanish poet Góngora, who was becoming the subject of new analysis. Of all this Lorca was acutely aware, but the effect of the currents on his own work was slow.

Himself a revivifying force in Spanish poetry, he was at first confused by these stimulating new currents. His first reaction was defensive. He said he could not talk about his own poetry. "And not because I am unconscious of what I am doing. On the contrary, if it is true that I am a poet by the grace of God, or of the Devil, it is also true that I am one by grace of technique and of effort, and by recognizing absolutely what a poem is." But "what a poem is" was then a changing ideal. Nor were the poets who were his contemporaries the only ones whose competition he felt. There was also the older poet, Don Juan Ramón Jiménez, whose vision of "what a poem is" had so fascinated him in his early days that the charge of being an imitator still haunted him.

The case of Don Juan Ramón was so special that his later fate should be recorded. Bearded, neurasthenic, greatly gifted, he recognized Federico's talent and gave him early place in his magazine *Indice.* In Madrid, writing in purple ink within a cork-panelled, soundproofed room, his eccentricities, like his arrogance, were part of his stock in trade. He had a tongue that was sharper than his poetry, and he ceded little to anyone. When he was old, and past caring, he was awarded the Nobel Prize, ostensibly for a poem about a donkey *(Platero y yo)* which every Spanish school child learned. His place in Spanish poetry was secure before he died, but his last years were hard.

Age and change did much to soften the earlier rivalry between the old poet and the young one. Romanticism was dying in Spain as in Paris. Newer currents (or older currents in a new form) moved the younger poets. Lorca's conversion from romantic ballads to surrealistic, Góngorist poetry of verbal beauty and great complexity of form and image was not the sudden thing it sometimes seems. Bit by bit he had been experimenting for years, hiding the new within the shapes of the old. Yet for most students of his work two events and the influence they exerted mark the change. The first was his meeting with the painter Salvador Dalí, and the second, his participation in the Góngora tricentennial celebration, held in Seville in 1927.

4

CHAPTER

Dalí, Love, and Góngora

THE LORCA-DALÍ FRIENDSHIP WAS, AS one might expect, instinct with thunder and lightning. Dalí was six years younger than Federico, the son of a Catalan notary who lived in a stone-built seaside house in Figueras—a town just north of Barcelona. In family and geography no two youths could have been farther apart than the *vega*-born Lorca and the sea-loving Dalí. Both were first-born sons, and spoiled, but showed very different results of that spoiling. Neither of them did well in school, neither acknowledged any attempt at discipline except by refusal and revolt. But whereas Federico always responded delightedly to affection, Dalí, from the time he could walk and talk, took pleasure in presenting himself as a self-centered and self-determining monster-child. Or at least that is what he says about himself. Whether his tales about his own atrocities are true, or merely designed to attract attention by shocking, is less important than that he revealed himself very early to be a boy devoted chiefly to drawing and painting. When he had clearly outgrown the opportunities offered by Figueras and Barcelona, his father and younger sister, Ana María, took him to Madrid so that he might engage in a contest which, if he were successful, would ensure his admittance to the Academy of Fine Arts.

As Federico had come to the *Residencia* under the guidance of Fernando de los Rios, so Dalí came with the sponsorship of the Catalan poet Eduardo Marquina, the man who had introduced Lorca earlier to the producer who put on his ill-fated first play. The usual presentations to professors and students were made, the usual whispers evoked by this strange-looking lad, wearing baggy trousers above gaiters to the knee and claiming to be a painter. "Then," writes Dalí in the snobbish phrases of the uncertain provincial that he was, "my father and sister went back to Figueras and I remained alone [scared, excited, lonely] settled in a very comfortable room in the *Residencia de Estudiantes,* a very exclusive place to which it required a certain influence to be admitted and where some of the sons of the best families were living." There, he says that he lived only for drawing, and during the first four months he spent only one peseta a day—outside, of course, of the all-embracing fees his father paid for him.

Federico and his friends discovered the stranger on a day when he left the door to his room open and his paintings visible. Excitement followed. Life for Dalí took on a new intensity of values. The two talented young men formed an immediate, if somewhat tense and competitive, friendship. Federico was the older by six years (in the post-adolescent years this represented a gulf) and with a reputation which, by the time young Dalí arrived, was woven into the very personality of the *Residencia.* With that advantage of years, the poet and his friends had become consciously the *avant-garde* of Madrid; the younger man both envied them and distrusted them. In his "Secret Life" Dalí describes them as "The artistic, literary advance guard, the non-conformist group, strident and revolutionary, from which the catastrophic miasmas of the post-war period [post-World War I, of course] were already emanating." This group included Pepín Bello, Luis Buñuel—already working with cinema, Eugenio Montes, who was greatly loved but little known outside Spain.

Having charged them with being swayed by tendencies more or less related to Dada, Dalí goes on: "Of all the youths I was to meet in that period, only two were destined to attain the dizzy heights of the upper hierarchies of the spirit—García Lorca in the biological seething and dazzling substance of the post-Góngorian poetic rhetoric, and Eugenio Montes in the stairways of the soul and the stone canticles of intelligence. . . . At the time I became acquainted with the group, particularly, they were all possessed by a complex of dandyism combined with cynicism, which they displayed with accomplished worldliness." He goes on to describe them as wearing British-styled tailored suits and golf jackets, with smartly trimmed hair regularly worked over by the barbers of the Ritz or the Palace Hotel, whereas he himself had put on velvet jackets and flowing bow ties of the style favored by Paris artists, and wore his hair long, tangled, flowing to his shoulders. It was five years later that Federico returned from a walk at Columbia University and declared in a poem, "I will wear my hair long." There is no testimony that he did.

Watching these extravagances from the distance proper to an older man, Moreno Villa of the *Residencia* staff remembers Dalí as "very thin, almost mute, closed within himself, timid, like a child who has been abandoned for the first time, or torn violently from his father and sister, bushy-headed, not very clean, always buried in reading Freud and the modern theorists of painting." The contrast with the older group of the *avant-garde* was spectacular.

With his customary arrogance, Dalí claimed that his new Madrid friends "possessed nothing of which I did not possess twice, three times, a hundred times as much"; later he says that they taught him to go on a "bender." On the other hand (and here is the interaction between the two young men as it appeared in Dalí's mind), "the personality of Federico García Lorca produced an immense impression on me. The poetic phenomenon in its entirety and 'in the raw,' viscous and sublime, quivering with a thousand fires of darkness and of subterranean biology, like all matter endowed with the originality of its own form." The artist's reaction to Lorca's force, as remembered twenty years later, was immediate: "I would do nothing that could not be clearly defined, nothing of which a contour or a law could not be established, nothing that one could not eat (this was even then my favorite expression), and when I felt the incendiary and communicative fire of the poetry of the great Federico rise in wild, disheveled flames, I tried to beat them down with the olive branch of my premature anti-Faustian old age [he was then twenty-two], while already preparing the grill of my transcendental prosaism on which, when the day came when of Lorca's initial fire only glowing embers remained, I would come and fry the mushrooms, the chops and sardines of my own thought."

This insistence on the definite and precise, on that which he could "eat," seeming so strange a note in the youth who is now the famous surrealist painter of fantastic images, had its effect on Lorca. He began to see the young painter not as the creator of pictorial fantasies which he has since become, not as the evoker of sensation which he longed to be from earliest childhood, but as an "hygienic soul" fleeing from the "dark tangle of incredible forms," a man who asks only "the ancient light that stands in front of things" as contrasted with that which sinks into the tangle of vines of the human heart. In his famous ode addressed to Dalí, (the translation is literal), the poet sees the painter as wanting,

> The fish in the fishbowl and the bird in its cage.
> You do not want to invent them in the sea or on
> the wind.

You stylize or you copy after having looked
With honest eyes at their small and agile bodies.

O Salvador Dalí, with your voice rubbed with an
olive's oil,
I tell what your person and your pictures say to
me.
I do not praise your imperfect adolescent brush,
But I sing the firm direction of your arrows.

I sing your beautiful striving for the light of
Catalonia
Your love for that which has a possible
explanation.
I sing your heart both tender and astronomic.
Plucked from a French deck, and carrying no
wound.

I sing the little siren of the sea who sings to you
Mounted upon a bicycle of corals and seashells

But most of all I sing a common thought
Which unites us in the hours both dark and
golden
It is not Art whose light strikes eyes with
blindness
It is first love, or friendliness, or fencing.

This poetic vision, appearing in the *Revista de Occidente* in April 1926, was more than a testimonial to the curious friendship that flamed between the two young men. It was Federico's first attempt at the ode form, and his first important excursion into surrealist poetry. No longer would he be content to write the sets of charming quatrains that still delight wide audiences. Now, his imagination led him into darker paths, to his controversial

"Ode to the Sacrament of the Most Holy Altar" ("Oda al Santísimo Sacramento del Altar") which roused the wrath of certain members of the Catholic Church, and his equally controversial "Ode to Walt Whitman" ("Oda a Walt Whitman"), a powerful but confusing poem which can be interpreted both as praising homosexuality and as decrying it.

The "Ode to Dalí" ("Oda a Salvador Dalí") has charm, even in a literal translation, but there is about it an air of the young prince patronizing an aspirant for his favor which tells more than do the words themselves of the uneasy relationship between the two men. Dalí, who was in those days the less secure as well as the younger, early felt this attitude of patronage and fled from it. . . . "I avoided Lorca," he says, "and the group which grew to be his, more and more. This was the culminating moment of his irresistible personal influence, and the only moment in my life when I thought I glimpsed the torture that jealousy could be. Sometimes we would be walking, the whole group of us, along the Paseo de la Castellana, on our way to the café where we held our usual literary meetings, and where I knew Lorca would shine like a mad and fiery diamond. Suddenly I would set off at a run, and no one would see me for three days."

The influence which the two men had on each other is evident to anyone who studies their respective poems and paintings. In a world which knows more of Dalí than of Lorca, which is prone to accept its artistic judgments through French eyes, which can read Spanish poetry only in translation but sees a painter's work without the interposition of such a barrier, it is easy to think that the Catalan corrupted the Andalusian and turned him from lyrics and ballads to a preoccupation with the dark and tortured images which fill the volume called *Poet in New York (Poeta en Nueva York).* This is only part of the truth;

in the light of Dalí's own statements, as well as of other accounts of their joint activities in Madrid, it appears the lesser part.

Both men were subject to the conflicting and disintegrating influences which swirled about them in Madrid, some of them coming down from France, from Germany, from England, from Russia. The forces of the *avant-garde* were literary, artistic, political; their constant aim, however dispersed in application, was to break up whatever had been accepted in the past and present the resulting rubble in new combinations and new forms.

Louis Aragon of Paris who, in a speech at the *Residencia,* attacked the "representatives of a dead civilization," and André Breton who also was one of the founders of the new artistic creed, claimed in words that echo today, that "the field was free only for a revolution, fantastically radical, extremely repressive, that extended to every realm." Starting in France, this revolution first infected painting and poetry; its primary point of attack was logic. "In language especially," says Maurice Nadeau, writing of the movement's history, "logic must be hunted down, beaten to a pulp, reduced to nothing. There are no more verbs, subjects, complements. There are words that can even mean something other than what they actually say. . . . Beauty, art have been the conquests of logic; they must be destroyed. Poetry must be 'soul speaking to soul,' dream must be substituted for 'directed thought;' images must no longer be the foxfire running on the surface of thoughts or feelings, but lightning flashes, continually illuminating 'the caverns of being.' "

Insofar as both Lorca and Dalí felt the impact of these influences they shared a common experience and might be expected to show similar reactions. But over and above this one must remember the very different temperaments on which these forces played.

To say merely that both men were artists influenced by the same surrealist era is to disregard the vital differences between them. It was Lorca who was the imaginative and inventive genius, whose "wild, disheveled flames" burst into a thousand images which in turn made their impression on the painter. Dalí could lead Lorca into the subterranean ways where psychiatrists were exploring man's dark subconscious—the painter spent much time reading in that field before he began to exploit it on his canvases. He could even use his position in Barcelona to persuade the Dalmau Galleries that Lorca's charming, and childish, drawings should be exhibited on their walls. But Dalí's own range of invention was essentially limited, and the catalogue of images he repeatedly employs is not large. He says himself that "the development of my mind and character can always be summarized in a few essential myths." In those days Dalí was a narrow and negative young man whose great technical skill was employed against a tremendous barrier of insecurity and frustration.

Federico, on the other hand, had hardly a negative nerve in his body. His mature life was one of bubbling energy. Not only did he exude music but his wealth of verbal invention was such as to win him titles hitherto applied only to such geniuses of Spanish literature as the great Lope de Vega himself. Such familiar stuff of romance as moons and myrtle, olives and oranges and gypsies, roses and fountains and red earth, horses and knives recur like themes of life itself in his early poetry. But if he later left such familiar symbols behind, it was not in a desire to imitate the painter's themes, but out of a more luxuriant tangle of invention. The student is far more likely to find the effect of Lorca's poetry on Dalí's canvas than to be able to analyze Lorca's wealth of imagery by reference to Dalí's artistic influence. Only when Lorca took awkward paintbrush in hand did the Dalí influence show, and then it was more Dada than Dalí.

The Lorca-Dalí friendship took on new dimensions outside the *Residencia.* However much Salvador in himself may have felt jealous of his friend's influence and popularity, he boasted of that friendship to his father, his mother, his sister Ana María in such glowing terms that in the spring of 1925 an invitation was issued for the Andalusian poet to visit the Catalonian family. The event was regarded as so important that the Dalís moved earlier than usual from dusty Figueras to their summer home in the sea-girt village of Cadaqués. Here they and their guest would spend Holy Week.

Federico, new friend of the son of the house, fell in love with the seaside village at once, and pronounced the surrounding landscape to be "eternal and perfect." The family responded with interest and affection. Salvador told them that his friend had written a play, and the friend responded by saying he would like to read it to them; he had never dreamed of doing it "in so intimate and welcoming an atmosphere." So, says Ana María Dalí, "amid the greatest silence and expectation in the dining room of the Cadaqués house, presided over by the baroque Virgin who looked at us, smiling, from her red velvet niche, we heard the reading of *Mariana Pineda.*"

This was the first play that Federico had gathered courage to write after the disaster of the ill-fated *Butterfly's Evil Spell.* A romantic tragedy, based on an historic episode laid in Granada, he had finished it in January 1925. The Dalí family was full of admiration. Señor Dalí, enchanted, said that Lorca was "the greatest poet of the century." Ana María found her eyes full of tears at the death of the heroine, and Salvador looked at them "curious and proud, as if saying, "What do you think of him?" and then looked at Federico who repeated delightedly his pleasure at their enthusiasm.

"From that moment on," says Ana María, "García Lorca was to my father like another son." He entered into the affairs of the house to such an extent that he came to take part in the slightest conflicts. And then this sensitive and intelligent woman, whose book describing Federico was published in Barcelona thirteen years after his death, makes her own assessment of the poet with whom she seems to have fallen hopelessly in love. Observing that someone had compared Federico to a swan, which out of water is heavy and graceless, but afloat is beautiful and radiates beauty all about him, she says of the poet that this was a true comparison. Outside his own ambience "which was to recite, to play the guitar or the piano, to talk about things that interested him, his face, otherwise hard and preoccupied, had an intelligent expression, full of vitality, but neither his square figure nor his rather heavy movements were attractive." But once he felt at home, he took on grace, and the whole person appeared "with a perfect elegance. Mouth and eyes harmonized so admirably that one could not remain insensible to his great attraction. The words flowed sharp and penetrating, and the intonation of the voice had great beauty. Everything about him was transformed. His presence actually embellished whatever surrounded him, as the swan embellishes the lake that reflects him."

"García Lorca had a great simplicity," she continues her assessment. "Although he certainly understood his own value, he never had the enormous pretension which always characterized my brother. Moreover, he was never open to suggestion. When an idea did not seem right to him, he would not let himself be influenced for anything in the world."

Life in Cadaqués was absorbing and enchanting. Salvador painted furiously, humming to himself "like a hive of golden bees." Lorca worked on a long poem to be called "The Sacrifice of Iphigenia" (this apparently has disappeared), when he was not walking or swimming with Ana

María. He loved the water, but he feared it. He would never go in by himself, and he was happier when holding onto the hand of Ana María, who swam like a fish and regarded this Lorca timidity with a somewhat oblique eye. "For nothing in the world would he go into the water unless we were near him. He feared that even the small waves would swallow him, or drown him. While he bathed, close to the beach itself, I had to hold him by the hand."

The lover, or the scared child? "Lorca's personality was so lively, so absorbing and attractive that we all felt impressed by him; moreover, he made himself loved by a spontaneously infantile trait. He wanted to be taken care of, to be constantly petted and pampered." (That early sickness, and his mother's devotion had left their indelible mark.) "He was afraid of dying, and with our hands in his, he was clinging to life. At times he suffered from throat trouble and his voice roughened. He wanted to be nursed, and not left alone for a minute. He asked for oil of eucalyptus, and his room was filled with its odor. He asked repeatedly for a thermometer. He would have liked us to give him many medicines, but as he had no fever, we limited ourselves to petting him. . . .

"The only time he seemed to have no fear of death was at mass on Sunday, when he found himself facing the idea of eternal life."

He was in Cadaqués in the spring of 1925; in the summer he went back with his own family to the *Huerta de San Vicente* on the Granada *vega.* There he wrote to Ana María that Cadaqués seemed to him "like a good dream" and he remembered "the slightest detail" of his visit. In the *Huerta de San Vicente,* which his father owned and where the family spent holidays, the house is big, surrounded with water and with fat trees, "but this is not the truth of it," there is also such "an incredible quantity of historic melancholy that it makes me remember the fair and neutral [a curious adjective, shedding an oblique light on Lorca family disputes] atmosphere of your terrace, where the visible grace of the air stands out."

During the next year or two Federico was in and out of Cadaqués. Dalí had a successful showing of his paintings in Barcelona, and Federico went to the Catalan capital for that. In October 1926 the artist, whose behavior, like his painting, had become more and more surrealist and, to more conservative eyes, more and more outrageous, was expelled, readmitted, and again expelled from the Madrid Academy of Fine Arts, the second time with such emphasis that the King's own name was signed to the edict. The artist and his sister then went to Paris, where he visited his fellow Catalonian, Picasso, and met the French leaders in the surrealist movement. Then they went on to Belgium, and then home. Federico came again and again. In between times he, who seldom wrote to other friends, sent wistful letters to Ana María, praising Cadaqués, remembering picnics and landscapes which both had enjoyed, telling her details of life in Granada.

Friendship with the Dalí family was clearly so important in Federico's life that one seeks for its root, its implications, its effects. "He was in love with Dalí" could be the answer. Or the answer might lie simply in the ample praise, the beautiful shore, the comfortable life and the petting which the Dalí family gave this man who was so often at odds with his own father. Or one might say cynically that Dalí and his friends opened literary and artistic doors in Barcelona which were valuable aids to Federico's ambition. All these are pertinent factors. So is the fact that the Dalmau Galleries gave his fragile surrealist water colors a showing in Barcelona which he could hardly have achieved in a commercial gallery in Madrid.

But there is still another possible answer, a normal romantic one which, in the face of modern insistence that Federico's so-called "defect" made its appearance early and was conclusive in his life and work, demands consideration. That Ana María was in love with Federico seems entirely possible. Testimony to such affection shines in her book wherever she writes about him, wherever she quotes his letters. She has never married, and she and her brother are not exactly "good friends." She never got over the breach which was opened between Salvador and the senior Dalí when the former painted "Blood is Sweeter than Honey" and his father ordered him out of the house. She carefully kept the letters that Federico wrote her so long ago.

As for Federico,—well, there are his affectionate letters to Ana María; some of them (demurely edited) are included in his *Complete Works* and some appear in Ana María's life of her brother. More significant, perhaps, is a letter which Federico wrote in September 1926 to his older friend, the poet Jorge Guillén (then teaching in Murcia), praising his poems and asking his advice. Federico was twenty-eight years old, Guillén was five years older, married, earning a living for his young family and writing poetry when he could. He and Pedro Salinas had both been scolding Federico for wasting his life, for remaining dependent on his family, in short, for refusing to grow up.

On September 2, 1926, a short time after that first visit to Cadaqués, Federico had written to Don Jorge asking his advice. He said he had *decided* to prepare for examinations for a professorship in literature "as I believe I have a vocation and the capacity for enthusiasm." He wants to be independent, "and to affirm my personality within my family. I had barely said this when my parents became very happy, and promised that if I began to study they would give me money to go to Italy, which I've dreamed of for years."

But how should he begin? Emphatically, *"I don't know how things are done.* . . . I neither eat nor sleep nor understand anything but poetry. And so I come to you. What do you think I ought to do to begin my preparation for a professorship seriously? . . . Yes, a professorship of poetry. What ought I to do? Where should I go? What should I study? What *disciplines* would be useful to me? Answer me. I am not in a hurry, but I want to do this in order to justify my poetic attitude."

Don Jorge must have answered quickly for Federico wrote a week later thanking him, and enlarging on his worries. "Should I work with someone? Should I go some place else? Should I go as a reader? . . . Will I have to wait long? This is important because I need to be located. Imagine that I might like to get married. Could I do it? No. And this is what I want to solve. I keep seeing that my heart seeks a garden and a little fountain as in my early poems. Not a garden with divine flowers and rich butterflies, but a garden with air and monotonous leaves where my five senses, domesticated, can look at the sky.

"Tell me about whether I can be a professor—or something! Don't think that I am *engaged* to any girl but could this not be imminent? my heart seeks a garden, etc. etc. (what etceteras, full of poetry and novelty!)."

What happened to this hinted romance? Was it real, or a pretense? (Don Jorge Guillén says it was only "a flirt.") Was Lorca seized with a sudden fright? Did something, perhaps a reminder of the effect of his early paralysis, persuade him that marriage was not for him? There is no evidence that Ana María jilted him, or that she ever had the chance to. But he did reveal to Guillén that family pressures toward a recognized "profession" were heavy. "My family gives me all the money I want and more, as soon as they see me on a road—how shall I say it—that is official!" The real source of Federico's misery and the family's pressures was that he could not seem to get oriented in life. To his father, this meant becoming self-supporting, and poetry would not do it. As Lorca told Guillén, "But for the first time they are opposed to my going on making verses without thinking of anything else." (It was not in fact the first time, nor the last time.)

Perhaps the heaviest pressures did come from the family. Perhaps that hint of romance was born of honeysuckle and tuberoses in the garden of his imagination. But, how is anyone to forget, or disregard, that coincidence of Cadaqués, Ana María, and the poet's plea to an older friend for help in getting the means for a garden?

The four years between 1924 and 1928, the Dalí years, were, for Federico, crowded with interest and emotional drive, but also beset with uncertain development and slow growth. Poetically, Lorca was trying to find his own authentic voice, not only in order to choke off the last of the critical charges that he was an imitator of Don Juan Ramón's romanticism, but also to find a new shape and a satisfactory vehicle for the creative drive that surged within him.

This struggle shows in the three phases of his developing work. The first was the charming simplicity of early poems in the *Book of Poems* and *Songs (Canciones),* which were pure singing, almost as clear and easy as the children's game rhymes which he loved and used to rewrite.

The second and third phases of Federico's poetry are, characteristically, confused in time, but very clear in substance. *Gypsy Ballads,* which both marks the end of the first phase and anticipates the second, was published in book form in 1928; the surrealist "Ode to Salvador Dalí" appeared in magazine form in 1926, yet in terms of poetic development the second antedates the first. *Gypsy Ballads* is in fact, if not in intent, Lorca's maturing farewell to the legends, the color, the passion, the romance of Granada. When these qualities appear later, it will be mostly in inverted, surrealist form, harder to recognize, but moved by the same intensive drive. The first of them, the ballad about Antonio Heredia, his trip to Seville and his murder at the hands of his cousin, Lorca had written as early as 1926, but publication of the whole group did not come for two years.

The delicious simplicity of the ballads is presented with a degree of sophistication which had shown itself very seldom in the earlier poems. It was for good reason that *Gypsy Ballads* was so wildly popular. The ballads were native to romantic Andalusia, flavored with gypsy life and death; strange to other provinces in Spain, they were accepted and loved as they were at home. A legend grew that they had been written by a gypsy, but the fact, of course, was that their author was not that. The poet was a lover of gypsies, their lore, their music, their vivid charm, a lover who lived on the more affluent side of the valley that divides the gypsy Albaicín from the Moorish-Christian heights of the Alhambra. The poems are easily and widely committed to memory, by all sorts of people from cab drivers to college professors; they even translate easily, and for hundreds of people in many countries Federico García Lorca is in person his gypsy ballads.

But the fact was not quite like the legend. Son of a wealthy landowner as Federico was, the myth that he was a gypsy disturbed him and his family, made him sound "lacking in culture and education," as he wrote Guillén. "The gypsies are a theme, and nothing more."

The poet's intention in the very different poems that represent his surrealist experiments first became public at the very moment when he was emphasizing his singing skill as the new minstrel of the old ballad form. This confused his friends and distracted his enemies.

Both aspects appeared in December 1927 when the *Ateneo* of Seville invited a score of Spain's younger poets to commemorate the tricentennial of the death of Don Luís de Góngora. That historic character was a famous but long-neglected poet of the 16th century whose baroque and complex manner of writing had fallen so far out of favor that, except in academic circles, even his name was almost forgotten. One of Lorca's friends, a poet and scholar named Dámaso Alonso, had found in Góngora's tortured verses characteristics which made them seem the forerunners of the new surrealist style that was drifting down from Paris. He spread the word that in Góngora, Spain had a neglected precursor of the fashionable new movement, and it was in the light of his enthusiasm that the tricentennial in the older poet's honor was organized.

For Federico, this was the second important cultural festival in which he had played a part. The first was the famous Granadan celebration of 1923 in honor of *cante jondo,* with Maestro Falla the leading figure, and Federico his enthusiastic collaborator. The second, the homage to Góngora, was organized and carried on by a group of young poets who were Lorca's contemporaries, friends, and competitors. The first had taken place in his home town, among friends who knew and loved him. The second was planned in a rival city, eager to hear him but skeptical of his fame. Each event drew from Lorca a preliminary essay on the subject under consideration meant to be delivered as a lecture on the appropriate night. Widely applauded, they added a new aspect of developing intellectual power to the poet's growing reputation. Both of them betokened recognition of his talents, both were preceded by intensive study and hard work.

Lorca had tried out his analytical essay on Góngora's poetry before an audience of his Granadan friends. They applauded as warmly as he had hoped they would. When he stood up before strangers in Seville to do honor to "the great and in his time greatly ridiculed Cordoban poet," it was with the confidence born of a successful rehearsal.

"Your professors, with rare and modern exceptions," he told his listeners, "will have told you that Góngora was a very good poet, who suddenly (and for various reasons) became a very extravagant poet [the usual phrase is that from an angel of light he became an angel of darkness], and that he carried language to the length of twisting meanings and setting up rhythms inconceivable to a sane mind." This Lorca denied, and cited Andalusian images in common speech which he said are truly in the same spirit which is "the spirit of the people," like the naming of a projecting part of the roof a "snare," "or calling a candy 'bacon from heaven,' or 'nun's sighs,' or naming a cupola 'half an orange.' "

"A poet," Lorca pronounced with the certainty of experience, "has to be a professor in the five bodily senses. These are—in this order—sight, touch, sound, smell and taste. In order to be master of the most beautiful images he must open doors of communication in all of these, and very often he has to superimpose their sensations on the other, and even to mask their natures."

And after this hint of measures familiar both to Góngora and to the surrealist that Lorca was becoming, the modern poet went on with a bit of analysis which contains the clue to many of his own images, however strange and arbitrary. "The interesting thing,"he told his audience, "is that Góngora, when handling forms and objects that are large in size, does it with the same affection and the same poetic grandeur as with small things. To him, an apple is of the same intensity as the sea, and a bee as full of surprise as a forest. He regards nature with a penetrating eye, and he admires that beauty of identity which is equal in all forms. He enters into what might be called the world which belongs to everyone, and there he proportions his sentiment to the sentiments which surround him.

"That is why an apple is to him the same as the sea, because he knows that the apple is in its own world as infinite as is the sea in the world to which that belongs. The life of an apple, from the moment of its coming into existence as a delicate blossom until it falls, ripe and golden, from the tree to the grass, is as grand and as mysterious as is the ceaseless rhythm of the seas. And a poet must know this. The greatness of poetry does not depend upon the magnitude of its theme, nor upon its proportions or its sentiments. One can make an epic poem out of the struggle which leucocytes carry on amid the prisoned branches of the veins, and one may give an endless impression of the infinite with no more than the form and fragrance of a rose." Or with the speaker's own poetic tragedy of a butterfly and a cockroach.

"Góngora measures all his material with the same yardstick, and as he manages seas and continents like a cyclops, so he analyzes fruits and objects. Indeed, the little things he enjoys with even more fervor." So did Lorca who, in one of his poems, called a lizard "a little drop of crocodile."

The proper applause followed, so did other proper speeches of homage. And then Lorca's cup overflowed. He was invited to read his unprinted *Gypsy Ballads* (known chiefly then to his friends in the *Residencia*). It had nothing to do with Góngora, yet so great a sensation did the group of ballads make that the applause outdistanced that which had been given his carefully prepared and much more pertinent lecture of homage. His listeners "went so far as to toss to him handkerchiefs and even coats, out of their Sevillian pride in his repeated allusions to the city and the river, the pastures and the marshes, the honor of Lower Andalusia. . . ."

A poet friend, Rafael Albertí, who was there says that in those provincial days and in terms of the ingenuous rivalry between the three Andalusian capitals there was nothing more surprising to them than that a poet from Granada should begin the recital of his ballad by putting on the road to Seville—and to see a bullfight—a gypsy from Benamejí, a son of the province of Cordoba. "Although García Lorca's poetic intention was pure, and alien to these local quarrels, the coincidence that he, a Granadan, should praise the sultry capital of the ancient Andalusian province set the Sevillians mad with joy." And then Albertí adds, like the true native of Malaga that he was, "So presumptuous are they [the Sevillians], so unbearably jealous of their city."

The festival had other elements beside fine poetry and high thinking. Albertí's story of the night, gay as it is vivid, holds the personal color and charm of those lost years. Demonstrations of friendship and "deep song" followed intellectual analysis and ballad rhythms. The part played that night by Ignacio Sánchez Mejías, the torero whose later death inspired Lorca's famous *Lament for the Death of a Bullfighter (Llanto por Ignacio Sánchez Mejías),* is as much a part of the poet's stuff of life as is Lorca's admiration for the famous singer of *cante jondo,* El Niño de Jerez. Ignacio Mejías, landowner and torero, was in fact the Maecenas of the festival.

During this visit, says Alberti's memoir, "García Lorca met the man who, with Sánchez Mejías, was the most extraordinary Sevillian of that period—Fernando Villalon Daoiz"—stockman, magician, theosophist, hypnotist, Count of Miraflores de los Angeles, and a poet whose first book, *Lower Andalusia, (Andalucía la Baja)* had just been published when its author was forty-eight years of age . . .

"Federico and Villalon became immediate friends, to their mutual surprise. In the afternoon the Count invited us on a trip through the city. Together we went through its intricate streets with their dangerous turns and windings in an absurd little motor car which Fernando himself drove. I shall never forget the terrified face of poor García Lorca, whose fear of automobiles was only comparable to that of Pablo Neruda—or to my own. For Villalon whirled in and out of alleys, dead-end streets, performing pirouettes and 'verónicas' that would have done credit to a bullfighter, and all the while explaining to us his future poem "Chaos" and taking his hands from the wheel the better to recite to us its first verses.

"When we met that night in Ignacio's country place, Pino Montano, in the outskirts, the shouts of laughter, the screams, the back-poundings, the gestures with which Federico related what had happened could have been heard in the Giralda . . .

"What a night, amid poets and good friends! We drank. We recited our poems. Dámaso Alonso, the great commentator on Góngora, astonished us by repeating from memory the 1091 lines of the poet's 'Primera Soledad.' García Lorca gave some of those amusing theatrical bits of his. And we all, even the Mephistophelian José Bergamín, ended sitting on the floor, huddled in Moroccan 'chilabas' which Sánchez Mejías himself had thrust over our heads." Even in sun-blessed Seville it can get cold at night.

"When that choir of drunken Arabs was at its most absurd, Ignacio announced the arrival of the guitarist Manuel Huelva, accompanied by one of those geniuses of *cante jondo,* Manuel Torres, better known as El Niño de

Jerez," who died poverty-stricken in Triana some months later. Immediately the 'deep song' started, with arguments in the intervals concerning the difference between the 'deep' and the 'flamenco,' the vihuela and the guitar. "The gypsy held us all entranced, caught by the throat with his gestures, his voice, and the words of his verses. He seemed a rough, wounded animal, a terrible well of anguish. But remarkable as was his deep voice, the most truly surprising element was his words, extraordinary verses of 'solares' and 'seguirillas,' complicated concepts, difficult arabesques.

"Someone asked him, 'Where did you get those from?'

" 'Some of them I invented, others I searched for.'..."

"Manuel Torres knew neither how to read or to write, he could only sing. But that he could do—his singer's sense was perfect. That same night, with a wisdom and sureness equal to that which a Góngora or a Mallarmé would have displayed in talking of his aesthetics, Manuel Torres confessed to us that he did not let himself go with the current, the too widely known, the well ploughed fields; then he summed up in a strange and majestic manner that which he thought we would understand—'In *cante jondo,'* he rumbled, his hands wooden on his knees, 'what one always has to look for, until you find it, is the black torso of the Pharaoh.' "

"As was to be expected, of all those present it was Federico who most praised this strange phrase of the Jerez singer. He was delirious about it. I realize now that no one in that magic Sevillian night found terms more precisely applicable to what García Lorca himself had sought and found in gypsy Andalusia, that he might make them blaze forth in his *Romancero.*

"That 'black torso of the Pharaoh,' which held for Manuel Torres all the anguish, the air of sentimental catastrophe, of a broad wound gushing pain and vague hatreds, is the equivalent of what, in Federico's best ballads, becomes that deep beat of misery, that hidden mist of drama, that thread never to be untangled so that the whole is cut, diffuse, lost, minus an end. The "Sleepwalking Ballad" ("Romance Sonámbulo")—"Green, how I love you, green"—is a good example of this. Lorca reinvented the dramatic ballad, full of secret chills, of mysterious blood. Whatever it was that happened in "Sleepwalking Ballad" or in "Black Sorrow" ("La Pena Negra") cannot be explained; it eludes all attempts to recount it. On top of the stones of the ancient Spanish ballad, Lorca, along with Juan Ramón and Machado, put a new one, rare and strong, at once to sustain and to crown the old Castilian tradition."

The influence of the Góngora festival went far beyond that magic night. The changes that neither Dalí nor Dada, nor the critic Guillermo de Torres had been able to force on Lorca, were brought about by this romantic dipping far back into the bottomless well of Spanish poetry. The lyric strain which had established him as the new sweet singer had not run out. But his inventions and his involutions—those verbal arabesques which he, brought up amid the architectural extravagances of the Alhambra, had touched gently or held back in earlier poems—now found the sanction of tradition. His strange "Ode to the Most Holy Sacrament" which was published in Ortega's *Revista De Occidente* in 1928, his controversial "Ode to Walt Whitman," his "Saint Lucy and Saint Lazarus" ("Santa Lucía y San Lázaro") which followed in a later issue of the same magazine, show the trend towards that neo-Góngorism which he would develop so much further when he got out of Spain.

Can this new strain in his writing be considered truly neo-Góngorism, or is it Spanish surrealism and related to the type that would appear on Dalí's canvases? In Lorca's poetry it is as native as it is effective. Competent critics have yet to analyze the effect of Góngora on Dalí, who is frequently described by critics as though his Spanish birth, childhood and youth had no effect at all on his painting. What Lorca thought about it is contained in his lecture on "The Poetic Image in Don Luís de Góngora" which he wrote before going to the Sevillian festival. He was, after all, first, last and always a Spaniard.

Between them, the two festivals mark a new phase of development in Lorca's life as in his work. In Granada he was secure in his accustomed role as the native poet and minstrel, the role he had played so often and so well at the *Residencia.* There he was surrounded by his friends. In Seville he was facing an audience of strangers, who by tradition might feel themselves alien, in that they were Sevillians and he was a man from Granada. But he won them as he had won smaller audiences in other places.

The taste of that triumph gave Lorca an added sense of confidence at a moment when he most needed it. After this lecture, he wrote his friend Jorge Guillén a very revealing letter. The lecture, he said, was very amusing for people "because I proposed to explain the *Soledades* so that they would understand them [those poems are very obscure] and not be 'brutos.' . . . And they understood! At least they said they did. I worked three months on that lecture. I will make you a copy and send it to you. As a *professor* you will tell me what idiocies were in it.

"But I was *serious.* My voice was different . . . serene and full of years . . . I have them." (He was then twenty-eight years old.) "And it worried me a bit to see that I am capable of giving a lecture without the people laughing at me. I am getting serious. Sometimes I have moments of pure sadness. Sometimes I am surprised when I see that I am *intelligent.* Old age!" He need not have worried about that.

If the festival in Granada had established Lorca as the gypsy's minstrel, the Góngora festival in Seville gave him a chance to think out and to expound his faith in the great baroque tradition. His espousal of the Góngora way sprang from many sources, including his own search for an escape from romantic lyricism which sometimes seemed to come too easily. That he should have had to find in the 16th century poet a durable justification of his own love of image-making before he felt able to move ahead into the perilous paths that were to lead to *Poet in New York,* and also to the great *Lament for the Death of a Bullfighter,* sheds an interesting light on a mind that exploded into poetry while it tended to hide its analytical intelligence.

Many people who love Lorca's songs and ballads, but find themselves unable to like his later poems, mourn that he ceased to carry his lyric vein into more modern adult themes. It is a criticism which does not stand much examination of the poet's life or of the period and place in which he lived. Songs such as his early ones represent youthful exuberance and the clear treble of untroubled voices. He had long dwelt at heart in a carmine tower on the slopes of the Alhambra. Already he stood accused, and with some reason, of staying too long in a spun-out adolescence. Moreover, the lyric vein was out of tune not only with his own tardy development, but also with the times. The air was troubled, and a world which was reading *The Waste Land, Ulysses* and André Breton in England and France had little patience with nightingales. Moreover, the song of love which might have given Federico's genius new wings was not his to sing. Fate had, for reasons which are still obscure, denied him that ecstasy; simple lyricism opened to him no new veins.

After the Góngora festival he continued to work on *Gypsy Ballads,* which he meant to make into an essentially Andalusian book, harmonizing the gypsy of mythology with the actual one that rode the *vega.* "The result is strange," he admitted, "but I think it has a new beauty." Earlier he had been working on what he then called his "didactic ode" to Salvador Dalí and on a long poem to be called "The Siren and the Carabineer" ("El Sireno y el Carabinero"). "It is a tragic idyll," he wrote Guillén, "the story of a carabineer who killed a sea siren with a single shot. At the end there will be a great weeping of the sirens . . . while the carabineers put the dead siren into the flag room. The whole with a great lyric impact. . . . It is the myth of the useless beauty of the sea."

Unfortunately only fragments of this latter poem exist. It seems to have been one of those good ideas dashed off at top speed in talking to a friend, but never given complete form, a characteristic kind of café table invention which went up like café smoke and left little trace. On the other hand, the "Ode to Salvador Dalí," without its limiting adjective, appeared in 1926 in the prestigious *Revista de Occidente.* And the *Gypsy Ballads* was finally published in book form in 1928. Both were exceedingly successful.

In the meantime Federico had written that puppet drama *(The Girl Who Waters the Basil and the Talkative Prince)* for the children's Christmas festival in Granada; this performance gave him a start in puppetry which he developed later. He was also continuing to write poems to appear in his volume *Songs;* he had his play *Mariana Pineda* finished early in 1925, though it did not reach the stage until 1927, and then in Barcelona.

In the two years which followed he made experiments in the neo-Góngorism that the tercentenary in Seville had inspired. "Saint Lucy and Saint Lazarus" appeared in the *Revista de Occidente,* and so did his "Ode to the Most Holy Sacrament"—both combined Lorca's old lambent lyricism with the older Góngorism or the new surrealism. He also adopted Góngora's title *Soledad* for a poem appearing in the magazine *Carmen* of Santander, one of the "little magazines" which spurred him to start *Gallo.* That he also published his very different gypsy ballads in book form that year merely added to the public confusion as to what this young genius was really trying to do.

Meanwhile, however, his fame continued to grow throughout Spain. His friend, the poet Jorge Guillén, older and better known, introduced him to audiences in the North. Guillermo de Torre, who was winning his spurs as a critic, started a new magazine, *Gaceta Literaria,* and invited him to collaborate. Federico, curiously, offered first to send him prose, and suggested his "Dialogue with Buster Keaton." Then he sent a set of poems with the request that the critic-editor "publish all of them, if it is possible. If not, omit what you like of the little ones . . . I think that on an Andalusian map it is hard to tell which of them have to be omitted." And then, as though in anticipation of a later adventure, he added, "Is it true that Nora Borges [sister of the famous Argentine poet] is with you? Tell me right away so I can send her some pictures of bulls which I am making."

5

CHAPTER

The Boy Grows Older

THE GÓNGORA FESTIVAL IN SEVILLE could be taken as marking the end of the Andalusian period in Federico's work, but that would be an illusion. The southern provinces of Spain in general, and the Granada sector above all, continued to be a constant source of life for him. Even when his parents followed him to Madrid and moved into an apartment there, he continued to return with them on holidays and in the summer to one or another of his father's properties on the *vega.* Andalusia might be "burning on all its four sides" in the summer, as he wrote Guillén, but it was home.

And Granada, its urban center, both charmed and irritated him. As Federico himself observed, "Granada loves the diminutive. And so, in general, does Andalusia. . . . The diminutive's only mission is to limit, to reduce in size, to bring within the house objects or ideas having a great perspective, and place them in the hollow of the hand. Boundaries must be put to space, to the sea, the moon, distance, and even to that prodigious thing—action. We do not want the world to be so big nor the sea so deep. We feel a need for defining their limits, for domesticating their enormous dimensions.

"Granada cannot sally forth from its house. It is not like other cities which sit by the edge of the sea or of great rivers, which travel forth and come back enriched with what they have seen: Granada, pure and alone, makes itself a little thing, binds close its extraordinary soul and knows no exit save toward the stars. Thus, having no thirst for adventure, it folds back upon itself and cinches in its size to fit its architecture. Thus the truly Granadan aesthetic is the aesthetic of the diminutive, the aesthetic of tiny things."

In 1928, the intellectuals and the artists of Granada were a small and close-knit group, conscious of their mission which was to keep the torch of culture burning in a city of eighty-thousand souls. This was no new undertaking. Granada was, after all, the seat of a Moorish culture that went back perhaps a thousand years. The sense of mission over the centuries continued to make itself felt. For Federico that mission at the moment was to waken Granada to the work of the new surrealist world. It would not be easy.

For if the intellectuals were traditionally content to be a highly rarefied group, seeming to live on spiritual as well as physical heights, the city itself had another and vastly different aspect. It is built on a dusty flat land spread along a narrow valley on top of a hidden river. On one side rises the hill called Albaicín, with narrow winding streets, houses "flung there as by a wind of hurricane force," and limestone caves where the gypsies live amid barking dogs and a furtive sense of fear. On the other side the smiling beauty of the Alhambra hill holds the red Moorish palaces, the gardens of the Generalife, the house of Maestro Falla and that of the English Consul of Federico's poem where his heroine Preciosa fled to escape the devouring wind and was brought milk with gin to drink. (There really was an English consul who lived there in 1928. They said that he put on his "smoking" to dine every night in solitary splendor after the English fashion.)

The hills dominate Granada in song and story and

appearance, but it is the sullen, dusty flat land that dominates it politically. For all its eighty-thousand souls the town had in 1928 no more than a single bookstore, and that only to serve the University. The level of literacy, as in all Andalusia, was very low. Its inhabitants were mostly small shopkeepers and artisans—pottery makers, cobblers, carpenters, cabinet makers repeating ancient and beautiful patterns in walnut and cedar, metal workers, girls who chattered all day over lace and embroidery frames. These were the people seen in the streets and heard behind the open balconies. They live in Federico's plays—Doña Rosita was his mother's friend, and the Shoemaker's Wife, like the lace-making sweetheart of Don Cristóbal, lived only a few streets away.

But if the people are gay and friendly, if songs still bubble out from balconies like rills of water down the hillside, individuals can also be suspicious, fanatical and at times dour. Granadans take themselves with an underlying seriousness which must be accepted by those who wish to live at peace with them. They do not like raillery at their expense. They were not likely to admire Lorca's newest venture, a magazine.

Federico's new enterprise, *Gallo,* was planned with great hopes. In obvious competition with other "little magazines," it was started with the aid of other poets. *Carmen* of Santander, *Litoral* of Málaga, under the direction of Federico's friends, Emilio Prado and Manuel Altolaguirre, had given space and provided audiences of his peers for some of Federico's individual poems. They also provided a forum for the contentious opinions of the young. It was entirely in keeping that Federico should want to establish a magazine of his own in Granada.

His ambition was never small. *Gallo* (Cock) was to be a big magazine, fourteen inches long and ten inches wide (almost as big as *Life,* then new in New York). It was to be printed on expensive glossy paper and to contain prose, poetry and advertising. Federico was its guiding spirit, and the man who must beseech his friends to send their contributions on time.

The first issue finally came out in February of 1928. Its stated price was one peseta twenty-five centimes. It had twenty-two pages of text, including an introductory "History of this *Gallo*" by Federico which declared itself the "ultimate legend of Granada," a poem by Jorge Guillén, a toast by Melchor Fernández Almagro, contributions from José Bergamín, Salvador Dalí, M. López Banus (who wrote on "Lucia in Sexquilandia"), and Enrique Gómez Arboleya. This intellectual fare represented the newest interests of Spanish youth in 1928. The magazine's commercial patronage—the advertisements that helped pay the printing costs—came from a combination of local interests (hotels, candy stores, embroidery shops) and foreign agencies doing business in Granada. Two of them, which to an American now mirror antiquities, were advertisements respectively from Goldwyn Mayer and from General Motors, the one calling attention to movies then showing in Granada, the other proclaiming the virtues not only of the Cadillac and the Chevrolet, but also of the now vanished Oakland and the La Salle.

The second issue, following in April, was culturally a bit more advanced in that it contained an "anti-artistic manifesto" adopted by "the most interesting section of Catalan youth." The text of the manifesto had clearly been inspired by the surrealist manifestoes out of Paris; it pictures the spirit of rebellious youth of the 1920s. "From the present manifesto," say the authors, "we have eliminated, in favor of our own ideas, all courtesy in our attitude. Any discussion with the representatives of present Catalan culture, artistically negative, though in certain aspects effective, is useless." They go on to eliminate not only all courtesy, but also all argument, all literature, all lyrics, all philosophy. They limit themselves to the most objective enumeration of facts. They affirm that a new state of post-machinist spirit is growing. They insist that "men of sport are closer to the spirit of Greece than are our intellectuals." They recognize some twenty-three elements that they accept (including jazz, movies, and modern poetry) and some sixteen that they denounce (including fear of the new or of ridicule, and the "ignorance of critics with regard to the art of yesterday and today.") Meant to *épater les bourgeois,* their declaratives still had a trace of the more positive attitudes that preceded them. This manifesto was signed by Salvador Dalí, Sebastian Gasch (to whom Federico wrote many letters) and Luis Montanya (to whom he dedicated poems).

Other contributions were equally characteristic of their time and their authors. Gasch (still a distinguished Catalan critic) had written for *Gallo* a critique of Picasso; three of the latter's paintings were reproduced. There was also a fragment of a novel in preparation by the poet's brother Francisco García Lorca (trained as a diplomat but doomed to teach in exile at Columbia University), a satirical account of *Susanna Emerging from the Bath* by Francisco Ayala (now a noted novelist) and two playlets, *The Maiden, the Suitor and the Student (La Doncella, el Marinero y el Estudiante)* and *Buster Keaton's Walk* (*El Paseo de Buster Keaton),* by Federico himself, as well as notes on various artistic events and a summary of the criticism which this iconoclastic young enterprise had created in Granada.

A third issue was planned, but it never appeared. The project was fun for those who were engaged in it, but it aroused jealousy among young writers who were not asked to contribute, and irritation among accepted contributors who too often resented being urged to get their pieces in on time.

As for the public, those who bought copies were interested, amused, but not as enthusiastic as were those who had made the magazine. Static, conservative Granada was touched, but not shaken. It had seen radical youth in other generations.

Federico nourished another idea which, had it come into being, might have been harder to disregard. This would take the form of a further jibe in the shape of a supposed successor magazine named *Pavo (The Turkey).* Presented in a sober gray cloak, it would pretend to be the protest of an elder against the shocking ribaldry of *Gallo.* This time the conservatives of Granada, who may have laughed behind their hands at the extravagances of the first performance, would surely have felt their pride involved. Had they taken the planned *Pavo* seriously as the retort of their kind against the impertinences of youth, they surely would not have found the joke a funny one. Luckily it got no further than the talking stage.

The "little magazine" fad flourished not only in Spain but in France, England and the United States. One is tempted to dismiss this contribution as merely a Spanish version of the international youth fantasia, but it was more than that. Granada in those days was a literal-minded small town whose sense of humor, like its fund of ideas, was both minimal and unsophisticated. There were residents who bitterly resented humor at their expense, and who were not going to forget *Gallo,* or its editor.

It was about this time that I first met the poet in Granada, and with him some of his friends. I was staying at a famous old hotel named for Washington Irving. An American pianist named Mendez, also there, had come down from Paris, and had brought with him a note of introduction from his teacher, the harpsichordist Wanda Landowska, to her friend Federico García Lorca. This note was bringing the poet up to the hotel to meet the pianist and read to him a few new poems. As a journalist and the only other American in the hotel, I was invited to share this experience. "You must have heard of him," the pianist insisted. "He is the most famous young poet in Spain today."

After dinner the "most famous young poet" came up the Alhambra hill with four of his friends who clearly believed that estimate of Lorca's position. Greetings and introductions were exchanged in the hotel lobby where he knew everybody. Then Federico, olive-skinned as a gypsy, black of hair and eyes, instinct with charm, led the way to a dusty piano in the "Moorish" salon, and began twisting up the velvet seat of the old piano stool. He would sing us a new poem in the old ballad form. It would tell about the young gypsy Antonio Heredia, son and grandson of the Camborios, a dreamy lad who had set out for Seville all alone at night to see the bulls, his only weapon a slim willow wand.

Lorca fingered a few chords, settled himself on the velvet stool, and began to chant the ballad. A chorded background provided the setting. His husky voice had warmth, color, and a certain magic attraction that made a foreigner feel the meaning even of Spanish words that had not been learned at school. As a performer he was superb.

Antonio, his ballad warned us, met bad luck as soon as he got out of town. The Civil Guard, questioning his presence alone on the road, refused to believe either his name or his peaceful intent. A son of the Camborios so gentle? Nonsense! So they put him into the *calabozo,* and in celebration of the arrest they all drank (this with a large smile) lemonade!

Once out of jail, Antonio started again, but again he had left his luck behind. Four jealous Heredia cousins, envying his crimson cravat, his lacquered shoes and his perfumed skin, crept up behind him. Four bloody blows attacked him, and he had to succumb. At the end, a weary angel put the gypsy's head on a pillow, and moaned, "Antoñito de Camborio, worthy of an Empress, remember the Virgin, for you are going to die!"

The ballad, tragic, was dimly ironic, with humor under the drama. This was a first version of what became a pair of ballads entitled "The Capture of Antoñito el Camborio on the Road to Seville" ("Prendimiento de Antoñito el Camborio en el Camino de Sevilla"), published later that year in Lorca's *Gypsy Ballads.* In gesture, tone of voice, expression of face and body, Lorca himself was the ballad. Degree of poetic ability could be judged later, but the actor's skill won instant command of his audience.

One more incident that May week added status and depth to the emerging image of this remarkable young man. Perhaps on the strength of the Landowska letter, perhaps because of our appreciation of his performance, Lorca invited the two Americans to the home of the composer Manuel de Falla the following Sunday afternoon. The man was internationally famous. We went along the Alhambra hill, around a corner to a white plastered house facing the valley before it. Church bells rang up from below. A piano sounded inside. The music stopped as the door was opened. A slender middle-aged woman stood smiling. "Señorita de Falla, sister of the Maestro, and the one who takes care of him," explained the poet. Everybody bowed, and Federico, clearly at home, led the way past a group of long-skirted women to the men waiting in the front room. White walls, dark furniture and rugs, another old upright piano, but this one was in tune.

The musician looked as slender as his sister. A short man, perhaps in his fifties, he was distinguished by a head as spare in back as the notable skull that shaped it. Two slender cords led to the shoulders below, in no way softened by excess fat. "*Es un santo*" was the local phrase about him, "he is a saint," and he looked it. This was a mystic and a martyr, as well as a musician; the strains of a whole lifetime showed in those tense neck cords. But the skull was broad and ample, and the slender face had room for humor as well as for wistfulness held in check by determination.

Federico explained that Falla would give his audience bits from his opera, "The Three-Cornered Hat," and this he did, playing the complicated score with small hands and square fingers that barely spanned an octave. Older men in the room fell silent, but while no one hummed or beat time, they were obviously following the music with the enthusiasm of people who knew it well. Meanwhile, the long-skirted women in the outer room whispered gently of life and death, marriages and babies. Such murmurings would have shocked most musical Americans, but they did not seem to bother Falla.

It became evident very quickly that Federico was not only a friend of the composer and a pupil, but was accepted as a member of the family, and was now engaged in showing off his master to new friends. The older man played in much the same way as his pupil had played, the back of the hand flat, the fingers stiff and not rising high. There was nothing remarkable about this piano skill except that it was the composer himself who was making use of it on music of his own composing. He played this music as simply as Federico had chanted his own poetry, with obvious skill and pleasure, if with an enthusiasm that was somewhat more mature.

Later there was talk about other matters—Lorca's magazine *Gallo,* his part in the Granada festival, in the Góngora tercentenary at Seville. There the matter rested for more than a year. The two Americans went their separate ways, watching for Lorca poetry in Spanish or translation, picking up bits of information about his past, his present, and his accomplishments, but getting no clear picture.

In the meantime something had begun eating at Federico. Perhaps fame did not come quickly enough, perhaps references to the influence of Juan Ramón Jiménez on his poetry still haunted him. His friends kept telling him that he was the greatest poet in Spain, but while he always welcomed praise, he had heard this from them too many times to make it capable of salving the ache that persisted.

The publication of *Gypsy Ballads* in July 1928, the preparation of a second edition of *Songs,* the magazine experience of *Gallo,* the plans for the production of his new play, *The Love of Don Perlimplín with Belisa in the Garden (El Amor de Don Perlimplín con Belisa en su Jardín),* might have seemed enough to satisfy a poet of Federico's growing stature, but something was torturing him.

In September he wrote to his Catalan friend Sebastian Gasch, "I am working with great love on things of very different kinds. I make poems of all kinds." He was also drawing. "If you like the drawings, tell me which one, or ones, you are thinking of publishing [Gasch was editing a literary art magazine called *L'Amic*] and I will send you the poems that correspond to them . . .

"Yesterday Dalí wrote me a very long letter about my book. . . . A sharp and arbitrary letter that poses an interesting poetic debate. It is clear that the *'putrefactos'* [the word means those who are rotten, putrid—this word which Federico is said to have invented was one of the epithets that the young of 1928 hurled at conservatives] did not understand my book, although they said they did."

And then the somber note, "In spite of everything, nothing interests me, or almost nothing. It has died in my hands in the most tender fashion. My poetry now moves toward another and still sharper flight. It seems to me a personal flight."

Later, he wrote again to Gasch, "I am sending you with this two poems. I hope they will be of the kind you like. They are in my new spiritualist manner, not linked with logical control, but with a tremendous poetic logic. This is not surrealism. The clearest consciousness lights them.

"These are the first I have done. Naturally, they are in prose because the verse is a ligature which they do not resist. But in them, if you will note, is of course the tenderness of my present heart."

He was drawing, indulging in prose poems, even posing as an expert in modern painting. This, like his drawings, stemmed from his many visits to Dalí and the submersion in artistic theory and practice which prevailed in that house. It would be pleasant to report that his education in those matters was thorough and his drawings satisfactory.

Gregorio Prieto, artist and friend, says, "In his poems he showed the painter; in his drawings he is less a painter than a poet." His pictures were imaginative, charming, but frail, lacking in artistic discipline, extremely sentimental. But Federico was proud of them, and they shed an interesting light on the poet's mental processes.

On the other hand, in March 1929 he delivered a lecture before the Women's Lyceum Club in Madrid on "Imagination, Inspiration and Evasion in Poetry" ("Imaginación, Inspiración y Evasión en la Poesía") which was brilliant. In the realm of words he was thoroughly at home, and growing in competence.

Talking of imagination, he told his listeners, "For me, imagination is the synonym for an aptitude for discovery. To imagine, to discover, to carry our bit of light to the shadowed region where all infinite possibilities, forms and numbers exist alive. Imagination fixes and gives clear life to the fragments of invisible reality where man moves.

"The daughter of imagination is the metaphor, born at times in a rapid blow of intuition, lit by the slow anguish of presentation.

"But imagination is limited by reality; one cannot imagine what does not exist; one needs objects, landscapes, numbers, planets, and they make precise the relations between them within the purest logic. One cannot jump into the abyss or dispense with real terms. The imagination has horizons, it wants to draw and make concrete what it embraces.

"The poetic imagination journeys and transforms things, gives them their purest meaning and defines relations which are not suspected, but it always, always, always operates on things of the most precise reality . . ."

How seriously he meant this explanation of the relationship between imagination and reality becomes evident as one follows his poetry into post-Góngora surrealism, which many readers have taken as his maddest expression. Actually, it is in many instances the most mature, most sane, the explicit, observant.

To support his argument about imagination and its objects he cited an "Ode to Sesotris" ("Oda a Sesotris"), "Sardanapolis," "The Academy of the Rose and the Inkwell" ("La Academia de la Rosa y el Tintero"). Unfortunately only the first of these has appeared. Perhaps lost in the Spanish Civil War, perhaps too strange to attract publication, only their names remain to tease his admirers. In December he took refuge in turning back to an earlier phase and gave a lecture on children's lullabies—a form that for years had interested him as a kind of folk song. The same month he was interviewed for a literary gazette, and he listed as the projects he had in hand more odes,

"The Three Beheadings" ("Las Tres Degollaciones"), *The Puppets of Cachiporra,* and his new play, *The Love of Don Perlimplín with Belisa in the Garden;* this latter awaited the production that had been promised, but its appearance was forestalled by the censor.

An older man might have borne this official banning with equanimity, might even have thought it funny considering its political source. Federico had neither defense. In spite of his passionate preoccupation with the theater, he had not yet made a successful mark on the Madrid theatrical world. *The Butterfly's Evil Spell* had been a youthful catastrophe, *Mariana Pineda* no more than a *succés d'estime.* Now *Don Perlimplín* was forbidden production, and the accompanying scandal had about it a touch of slime.

Whether it was this which bit into his soul, whether one of the practical jokes played with Dalí had brought him disapproval that stung, whether some internal crisis submerged him in melancholy is not quite clear. Outwardly his star was unaffected. His poems had a widening circle of admirers. The reputation as a critic which he had established in Granada and Seville he improved in Madrid with his lecture before the Lyceum Club. But something was wrong.

As to what this something was, his constant companion in those days, Martínez Nadal, writes, "As the months passed and the popularity of *Gypsy Ballads* increased the poet felt the weight of his own work. This, with certain personal reasons [never explained], thrust him into the only period of depression in his existence. He turned sad, sought to be alone, ceased to talk of his plans, and strangest of all, stopped reciting his poems in public."

The poet's return to Granada in the spring of 1928 and his experiment there with *Gallo* was perhaps a form of escape.

Certainly successful poetry was not enough, even when Federico was drawing more than incidental expressions of praise for himself. That second half of his being, the theater, still cried within him to be given voice.

His early reputation as a minor provincial poet writing gaily of children and gypsies continued to dog his footsteps; this he resented and did his best to counter. Unfortunately for the family peace of mind, that countering process did him more harm than good. His new surrealist poems were not only harder to read, less pleasant, much less popular than the songs and ballads, but their language was sometimes offensive to the conservatives who refused to be convinced that to be recognized as a modern poet was a worthy goal. There was even a rumor that certain influential members of the Catholic Church sensed heresy in his "Ode to the Most Holy Sacrament," and were adding their discreet but very real pressure to his other woes. Moreover, his association with the theatrical world of Madrid was tinged with scabrous rumors; hints of homosexual relations there hardly redounded to his credit in the conventional world of Madrid society in 1928–29.

Moreover Federico's funds were continually scarce; he was not yet a dependable earner, and his family kept him mostly on short rein. He gave no sign of having paid further heed to his father's desire that he become a lawyer; the older man found no pleasure in his poems.

In addition to these professional difficulties there were rumors of trouble in his own love life. One must move with caution in this realm; gossip of 1928–29 becomes in some instances accepted "fact" with the changing years. Yet in the record there survive those indications of involvement with the Dalí family; when Salvador and his sister went to Paris in 1929, and reported it more receptive and challenging than Madrid, a corrosive coolness developed between the two men. And how is one to regard those continuing passionate dreams of having a garden, his plea to Guillén for help in becoming a professor—short dreams, perhaps, an empty plea, but at the moment clearly from the heart?

A French critic who years later wrote an account of the poet's life says of Federico that "tormented since 1926 by a crisis—or better, a series of sentimental crises which culminated at the end of 1928 and start of 1929, the poet imposed on himself as a rule, joy at any price!"

Perhaps he did. Certainly the series of parties in which Federico is described as singing, reciting, talking from mid-evening until dawn represent a kind of joy, though at this distance it may sound feverish and wearisome. It was a joy that showed all too plainly a mind corroded by torment. The best account of the undisciplined and frequently irrational excesses to which Federico was driven after 1929 by the "passion which I must conquer" is contained in the portions of a diary kept by the Chilean diplomat Carlos Morla Lynch, who had suddenly become Federico's intimate friend and confidant.

Unlike Lorca, the Chilean kept a diary, a remarkably detailed dairy, and after the poet's death he was "persuaded" that "at times it was sensible to reveal the true entity of great men." So he picked out of his diary evidence of the Federico "who comes and goes, who laughs, who sings, who recites poems and is lit up, who picks up the guitar or sits down at the piano, who is exalted, becomes passionate, is angered and moved, grieved and saddened." This is written with little reference to the past and none to the future. Here is the "strict present" of the critical period from November 1928 until the spring of 1929 when the poet took the extraordinary step of leaving Madrid for New York. Here, if any place, one might expect to find a fresh light on the "passions which I must conquer" that Federico mentioned to Gasch.

What one gets from the Chilean's excerpted diary is an impression of charm, gaiety, and complete irresponsibility, almost to the point of incipient madness. The beginning of the friendship was like a farce. In the small intellectual circles of Madrid it became known that the new Chilean Ambassador was a person of taste and charm who had read Federico's poems and wanted to meet the poet. The reply was that Federico would like to meet the Ambassador. Hours were named by mutual friends eager to act as go-betweens. Nothing happened.

By this time the poet seems to have tossed away all response to discipline except that involved in the writing of his poetry. Time, which had seldom imposed on him a strong sense of order, lost all power with him until night became for his purposes the same as day. He, who as a youth had been so meticulous in his dress, turned careless. He came and went as he pleased, disregarding any request from any friend that he arrive at this hour or that. Morla Lynch's account of their meeting is characteristic of the personal anarchy that by then had become the poet's increasing practice.

Federico was amiable, but elusive. One friend and another tried to bring about the meeting. One friend and another assured Morla Lynch that Federico wanted to meet him. Nothing happened. Other friends kept telling the diplomat that the poet would come to see him. Hours were named, and passed without the promised visit. Once, Federico got half way up the stairway, and ran down again. Finally, he was heard at the door itself, and that time Morla Lynch opened it before there should be another disappointment.

A wonderful sense of acquiring a new friend on sight overcame them both. They clasped hands, Federico with "that magic laugh of a permanent child." "Why was it so hard for you to come?" asked the Chilean. "I was afraid, because I did not know . . . ," answered the Andalusian, leaving the sentence incomplete, but understood. The two men talked. Hours went by; it was six, seven, eight. At ten, a customary Spanish dining hour, they dined, and talked some more. Midnight came and went. At three in the morning Federico moved to another chair, and announced that before he went—and he apologized for going so early—he would sing the song about the death of the burro that carried the vinegar for the village. He sang it, then he left, then came back for a package he had never brought. The friendship was established.

After that Federico came and went as freely as a member of the family, "almost daily, without any fixed program. He came and went, stayed to dine, or to sup,—or both things—slept during the siesta hour, sat down at the piano, opened it, sang, closed it, read us a poem, went, came back again. . . . He brought with him vitality, animation and optimism. . . . The magic which Federico radiates when he sits down at the piano is inconceivable."

So much for those hidden passions. But if the new Chilean friend did not take them seriously, the Lorca family did.

For a combination of reasons they worried and they held councils. What to do with Federico, what to persuade Federico to do, and how? Finally there came a gleam of light. Professor Fernando de los Rios, friend and mentor who had first taken the musician-poet to Madrid, was to lecture in New York that summer at an interesting institution called the New School for Social Research. Why should Federico not go with him, study English at Columbia University's summer session, widen his vision of the world, enlarge his circle of friends, improve his reputation and—though this was not so openly said—escape from the miasma of Madrid, the critical clash, the gossip and the unkind rumors that haunted him (and his family) in Spain? The decision was made, and made public when the poet wrote Morla Lynch in June, saying simply that he had "recovered his serenity" and for a change of air had decided to go to New York. The family would approve that, not warmly, but enough to give him a minimum of money.

Days passed, Federico went to Granada. Later, on the street, someone pounded the Chilean Ambassador on the shoulder. Lorca, back from Granada, was about to start for New York by way of Paris and London. And after he went, Morla Lynch makes one illuminating reference to the other side of Federico: "The fear of life. Always that deep obsession which lives continually like a shadow in the midst of his optimism and gaiety. That fear of the 'unexpected,' of that threat of what can happen suddenly and change the course of our existence."

He said to Federico, "But changes can be favorable." The poet shook his head, "Those are hopes for the unhappy. For those who do not want it, because they are happy, the idea of an unexpected change is a tragedy." And the Chilean comments, "Life cannot be always content, as he cannot be always sane, happy, optimistic and free of apprehensions . . . because there cannot be light without shadows."

Later, Federico wrote Morla Lynch from shipboard that he felt "depressed and full of homesickness. I am hungry for my country and your little salon. Nostalgia for talking with you and singing you old songs of Spain. I don't know why I left, I ask myself that a hundred times a day. I look in the mirror of the narrow stateroom and do not recognize myself. I seem another Federico."

6

CHAPTER

Introduction to New York

THAT "OTHER FEDERICO" HAD STARTED out with his friend and mentor in the traditional Spanish way; those taking a transatlantic journey from Madrid in those days usually began by a train trip to Paris. With Lorca and de los Rios went, for part of the trip, the professor's young daughter Laura, who had played a part in the Granada *cante jondo* festival. There was also an American student friend of Federico's whom he had met in Madrid; this was Philip Cummings, who would play an important, if short-term, role in the poet's life. In a dusty second-class carriage of the old traditional European type, the two young men sat up all night, talking most of the time, stopping only for awkward bits of slumber.

The young American left the party in Paris and headed for Switzerland and Sweden; he carried with him a promise that Federico would visit the Cummings family at a camp in Vermont once his summer studies were finished. Another friend, writing a quarter of a century later, reports that the poet and his older professor friend went to Oxford, Scotland and London before embarking for New York. In Paris, Federico was impressed by the Louvre. In London, he remembered only the British Museum and the lights in Piccadilly. His mind was back in Spain.

The city for which they were bound was to be strange to Spanish eyes, not only in visible bulk and extension, but also in its characteristics and its attitudes. Of it he knew very little more than that New York was at one and the same time blazingly rich, and bound into the frustrations of a law forbidding any drink that was alcoholic.

He may also have remembered that New York audiences had not been thrilled by Falla's puppet opera which Federico had helped to stage in Seville. *El Retablo de Maese Pedro* had been played in New York's Town Hall in 1926, with a cast composed of two sets of puppets, one set life-size and the other the regular size of marionettes. Its audience was more puzzled than enthusiastic. Olin Downs, then the distinguished music critic for *The New York Times,* said of it at the time that the puppets were amusing but distracting, that "the big puppets were not nearly as effective as the small ones, and they did not coincide with the contrasts of feeling in the music, for De Falla, in a remarkable score, has clearly differentiated between his puppets and his humans. . . . *El Retablo* furnishes a score in which De Falla has wrought with extraordinary fineness of touch and deftness of hand. . . . The music is Spanish, racial without being a mere retelling of popular idioms. Simple as it often sounds it is actually a tour de force." And he ended by saying politely, "The evening in the main cast much credit upon the enterprise of the League of Composers" which had been responsible for the New York presentation "and gave the listeners a new and valuable perspective upon perhaps the most important living Spanish composer, Manuel de Falla." In other words, the music was lovely but the production was a flop. If insects did not make good theater, puppets did not make good opera. The city had not welcomed Falla, would it welcome Lorca?

But for the moment this was background. Everything

about New York at first sight was strange except the weather; when Federico's ship landed it was full summertime, hot as Madrid, hot as Granada, and at times with a damp heat worse than either. He and Professor de los Rios arrived by ship on a morning in early July, and if Federico was at that time stirred by the beauty, the power and the terror of Manhattan looming in the misty dawn, he failed to record it.

At Columbia University the two visitors had friends—the learned and argumentative head of the Spanish Department, Federico de Onís, and Angel del Río, the gentler, younger scholar who would succeed him. Both were Spaniards; both knew Federico's reputation as a brilliant young poet; both were friends of Don Fernando. Both would befriend the new arrival. Under their guidance Federico, knowing no word of English, stood in line to register for a summer session which would begin July 8th. Before and behind him were all the motley crew, old and young, American and foreign, who for six weeks would be his fellow students; some of them were pupils bent on making up failed courses, others were teachers taking extra credits to help in establishing their careers in the academic world. Most of the process and the spectacle, even the little he understood, must have seemed extremely queer.

It was agreed that every morning at 11:30 he would take a class for beginners in English, a course taught by a Miss Amy Shaw and described as being designed "for educated foreigners who have practically no knowledge of spoken English."

Classes started July 8th and would end August 16th. For lodging, Federico was first assigned a room in Furnald Hall, then in a tall building called after the diplomat John Jay. He had a corner room that looked across lower buildings at Riverside Park and the Hudson River. Here he could have studied fruitfully, if study had been his strong point. But he had never been happily a student in terms of examinations passed and points earned; now he was past the student stage. English words were not the ones that would sing themselves in his mind. He was a Spanish writer, a poet and a dramatist, and Spanish poetry, prose and drama were what occupied him at the student's desk in the corner window of his room.

If the order of poems as printed in the volume *Poet in New York* is significant, the first one he wrote is the "Return from a Walk" ("Vuelta de Paseo") in the section "Poems of Loneliness in Columbia University" ("Poemas de la Soledad en Columbia University"). Of his loneliness this leaves no doubt. In spite of the green beauty of Columbia's campus, in spite of the park and the great river at the foot of 116th Street's hill, in spite of the poet's charm, his facility in making friends among the small group of Spaniards who knew what he had done and gave him abundant welcome, he was first of all homesick. And it showed in his poetry.

At Furnald Hall, his immediate neighborhood was the campus of Columbia University. True, a hill lay below, but it was not the Alhambra hill, or the hill of the *Residencia.* The hill ran to a river, as did his hill in Granada, but it was not his river. So in his own private code he wrote in "Return from a Walk" of the hot sky and the anonymous shapes that go toward the river, of the pollarded trees "and the egg-white face" of a blonde child, of the little toy animals with broken heads that children left on the campus, and of his weariness, deaf and mute as he felt himself. That first poem is not a happy one.

Knowing the neighborhood, the climate, the things that were around him as he wrote, this poem can be put into simple English phrases. They do not make poetry, but rather the kind of literal translation which Dámaso Alonso made in 1927 of the *Soledades* of Góngora. "Murdered by the sky," (New York in July is bright and hot) "with the pollarded tree that does not sing" (because it has only stumps where former branches moved).

> with the little broken-headed toys
> and the ragged-edged footprints left by dry feet
> walking careless through puddles and then
> stepping on to dry pavement
>
> with everything that fatigue has made deaf and
> dumb
> stumbling along with my everyday face so
> different
> from those around me
> and the butterfly drowned in the inkwell
> murdered by the sky.

He wrote many other poems at that corner desk, and he may have started *Don Perlimplín* there, though he must have finished it at another desk in another building.

The happiest thing he did in those six weeks was to assemble a chorus in Columbia's Spanish Institute and teach them Spanish folk songs. In its lesser way, the Spanish Institute at Columbia filled for him the place occupied by the *Residencia* in Madrid. It had a library of Spanish books, a big meeting room, a piano. Its members were mostly Spanish-speaking students, and here they had space for talk and laughter. Out of their number, the homesick Andalusian gathered enough singers to make a chorus. On August 7, 1929, in the last week of summer session, the chorus gave a concert of popular songs. A Cuban danced, and so did a beautiful young Ecuadorian who had studied in Seville. A program still extant shows the Director of the Chorus of the Institute to have been Federico García Lorca.

That was forty-eight years ago, and the members of

that chorus, like the members of that summer session, are scattered across the world. One of them, Ella Wolfe, recent widow of the writer Bertram Wolfe, remembers Federico's dark and smiling charm, and the gaiety of rehearsals of his chorus. She and her late husband were both students of Spanish, and eager to get, in six weeks, all of it that they could. When the autumn term began that year they registered for a popular course that the late Professor de Onís gave on *La Celestina,* alive in Spain's Golden Century. At times Federico listened. So did Julio Camba, a visiting Spanish humorist, so did a beautiful Spaniard named Antonieta Blair. "Three nights a week we all met in class, and after class we walked around the campus and talked—talked of many things, with plenty of laughter."

Antonieta ("one of the most beautiful of Spanish beauties") took all this gay companionship very hard. She was said to be married to an Englishman in Mexico, but to have grown disenchanted with him. The report is that she fell in love with Federico, got no instant or adequate response, stayed around hopefully for six months longer. To at least one friend she insisted passionately that Federico was the greatest dramatist since Molière. But if, as might be assumed, she wanted to shed her rich husband and marry Federico, neither he nor fate consented. In the end she is said to have gone to Paris and, kneeling before her favorite saint in Notre Dame Cathedral, to have killed herself. The act created an open scandal; the church had to be closed for three days while the priests wiped out the stains in a ceremony of purification and reconsecration.

None of Federico's poems written at Columbia show much sense of contentment. The process of being a student did not interest him. As for lectures, by this time he preferred the giving rather than the receiving of them. In spite of his admiration for Shakespeare, he showed no interest in the dramatist's language, no knowledge of its word meaning, its sounds, no feeling for its nuances or its richness. In a musician, this inattention was curious, but his friend Gabriel Maroto, printer and painter, who had taken Federico's first sheaf of poems away from him and published them in book form, may have had the key. "His thoughts in Spanish are too important for him to waste time on another language," said Maroto flatly. But that was later, in the winter. Meantime the summer session was ending and ahead lay the rest of a long, hot New York summer for the poet-dramatist to endure.

It was under these circumstances that Federico remembered the young American, his friend Philip Cummings, who, on the way from Madrid to Paris, had invited him to go to Vermont.

7

CHAPTER

Interlude — Federico in Eden

OF ALL THE MYSTERIES ATTENDANT on what Federico did and said, perhaps the most curious is that persistent one which for nearly forty years has surrounded his visit to Vermont. His biographers assert that he went there for ten days in August 1929, immediately after the end of the summer session at Columbia University where he had spent the usual term of six weeks—or that part of it which could be spared from his roaming about New York City. They do not go further, yet this Vermont visit was his first introduction to the country life of the United States. Out of it came two sets of clearly identifiable and very important poems—"Poems of Lake Eden Mills" ("Poemas del Lago Edem Mills") and "Poems of Solitude in Vermont" ("Poemas de la Soledad en Vermont"). These first appeared in 1940, four years after Federico's death, as part of his volume *Poet in New York.* They came to the casual reader's notice in English translation, and then (in Mexico) in Spanish.

Yet no account of his visit to Vermont has ever appeared in his biographies. His friend and biographer, the late Professor Angel del Río, writing in 1955 an introduction to the new translation of *Poet in New York* which Ben Belitt had made, repeated what he had said earlier, that

"Federico went to Vermont to visit an American friend. This was a fellow-poet, according to him, a Mr. Cummings, whom he had met a few months before in the *Residencia* at Madrid. This friend, I regret to say, I have never been able to identify; and if he was indeed a poet, he would have been Lorca's only contact with a creative American writer during his stay in this country." The second part of that statement is as questionable in point of fact as the first.

Federico, Professor del Río went on to explain, left Vermont after a few days to visit him and his wife at a farm in the Catskills near Shandaken which they had rented for the summer, and then to stay with Professor Onís at Newburgh. That the poet should not have identified his American friend more clearly, should not have told either of his Spanish friends about his ten-day visit with this American family, should not have talked at all of the wild Vermont countryside over which he and his host had tramped, and about which he wrote obliquely, is hard to believe. One can only fall back on characteristic suppositions, such as failure of memory on the part of the professors, or the customary Spanish disregard of people and facts that they dismiss as not concerning them. Was it that, never having heard of this Mr. Cummings before the visit, or from anyone else but Federico, the older men dismissed the American friend as a somewhat dubious reality, one of those characters that Federico had perhaps invented? Or was there a darker fear that something had happened during the visit, or in connection with it, that made a more extended account of it something that was better left unexplored or unrecounted?

Whatever the reason for this peculiar and extended silence, the facts of Lorca's Vermont visit have now emerged. And they have emerged not out of hidden documents or after extensive research, but because somebody knew somebody who knew somebody who took part in the drama. Federico's American friends are still legion, and a great many of them keep small gems of knowledge about him which stay gleaming in the mind. Among those gems was the name of his Vermont friend.

Philip Cummings—"Felipe" to Federico—is a tall six-footer, white haired now, but as vigorous and as completely of Vermont as he was when he and Federico ranged the hills around Lake Eden, climbed Mount Morris with the "Boy Stanton" and bathed in the crystal lake. His occupation is that of economic consultant to oil and mineral interests the world around. He has been married for thirty-odd years to a delightful woman, born Cornelia Weston. Their charming old white house (built in 1764) stands at the end of a dirt road.

In other words, the mysterious and potentially suspect Mr. Cummings is and always has been a substantial Vermonter, son and grandson of Vermonters. He was born in Hardwick, Vermont. His school years were spent there, and his undergraduate years in Florida. His interest in Spanish came first, he says, from Galician stonecutters, whom he, as a boy, saw cutting stone in Hardwick; this interest was deepened in Florida, and when in 1929 he was graduated from Rollins College he went to Madrid for further study. This he continued with a scholarship from the Institute of International Education.

It was in Madrid that he met Federico as so many other people met him, pouring out music at a piano in the *Residencia.* Cummings' Spanish was fluent, and his love of both music and poetry very real; these formed instant points of contact. He was some six or eight years younger than Federico, but in those days Federico was of any age he liked. Interested in people, sensitive to new friendships and possessed of an immense subconscious system of antennae that brought him the feel of people ("discerning sensitivity" is Cummings' phrase for this facility in the poet), Lorca took him as a new friend. They ranged the Spanish capital together, pushing down into the old town behind the *Rastro,* walking endlessly fascinating streets (this was a favorite diversion in those days before the motor car ruined it), discussing everything under the summer sun or the winter moon.

Cummings, who supplemented his scholarship money with teaching and translating, was introduced by Federico to Margarita Xirgu, who played principal roles in so many of the poet's plays. He went at least once to Granada, where Federico showed him not only the town but also the glories of the Sierra Nevada, as Philip was later to show his friend the very different beauties of Vermont's Green Mountains. He met Federico's mother, a sister, some gypsy friends. And when Federico, with Professor de los Rios and his daughter Laura, set out for New York, it was this Cummings who travelled with them from Madrid to Paris, then took his own way to Scotland and Switzerland, and got home in July.

Cummings was a good Vermonter, and as proud of his own wild and beautiful country as Federico was of the beauties of Granada. When in 1929 he learned that his Spanish friend was coming to the United States, he wrote inviting the young Spaniard to visit him in Vermont. Cummings had been teaching that year, and with his own earned money, he rented a place at Lake Eden where he could give his mother a rest in her own native countryside. This place was a simple two-story cabin on the edge of the lake. It is still there, and thanks to some unknown spirit with an extra-sensory perception of the past, it now bears the Spanish name "*Mañana.*"

Here the Vermonter proposed to entertain his friend the Spaniard. Knowing that Lorca's Spanish resources were slender in terms of United States dollars, the invitation included the check to pay train fare. Federico, who had reached New York in time for the July 8th beginning of the 1929 summer session at Columbia University, replied promptly in a letter that characteristically has no date, but gives internal evidence of having been written in July, shortly after his arrival in New York and his registration at Columbia:

"My dear little friend," he wrote in Spanish, "I received your letter with great joy. I have already found a place in New York. I want to see you very soon and I think continually of you, but on the advice of Professor de Onís I have matriculated in Columbia University, and for this reason I cannot go to you for something like six weeks. If you then continue to want me, I will be enchanted to go to you.

"If you are then no longer in your house, I beg you to come to see me in New York.

"Is this all right? Write me with complete frankness whether this is possible."

And then, "I am embarrassed by your great kindness in sending me the money for the ticket, and if my trip cannot be arranged within six weeks, I will send it back to you, always with that gratitude and noble loyalty which is the very best that a Spaniard can give.

"Write me at once, dear friend, and tell me if this delay in my trip is all right.

"I hope that you will answer me and will not forget this poet of the South, lost now in this Babylonic, cruel and violent city which is, on the other hand, full of great modern beauty.

"I live at Columbia, and here is my address.

Mister Federico G. Lorca
Furnald Hall
Columbia University
New York City

"I hope you will answer me immediately.
"My respectful greetings to your parents.
"Farewell, dear friend, and with an embrace from,

Federico"

Philip's reply to this eager and wistful letter has not survived the years, but apparently the six weeks delay presented no difficulties. At the end of Columbia's 1929 summer session, during which Federico had learned a great deal about New York but very little about the English language which he avowedly had come to study, (the session closed August 16th) he was taken by a friend to Grand Central Station and put aboard an early morning train. His destination was Waterbury, Vermont, which he would reach some nine hours later, and where his host would meet him.

Del Río, knowing about the adventure if not about the host, writes that Federico, about to be left in a strange train for a nine-hour journey, and knowing no English, "was genuinely worried by his removal from all means of communication. He dramatized the incident by shouts and gestures until the friend who had taken him to the train assured him, after talking with the conductor, that he would be left safely in Vermont."

At New Haven they left the shore and turned northwest, reaching Springfield about noon, and White River Junction (then a populous railroad town) in Vermont late in the afternoon. Tired as any traveller after an all-day trip, he was guided out of the car at a small town named Waterbury and into the welcoming arms of his American friend. Joyfully the two exchanged Spanish *abrazos,* pounded each other on the back, picked up Federico's luggage and started north with the Cummings family's Model T Ford. For the first time since early morning the young Spaniard could talk his own language and be understood. Full of comments and questions, both young men talked at once, and then settled down to the serious business of driving home along a sunset road. In mid-August, daylight near the Canadian border does not last late, and they had thirty winding miles to rattle over before they reached Lake Eden.

The way to the lake slides out of the rolling hills near Waterbury, then turns and twists along steeper ways where the pointed firs rise like candles above the mass of green. Federico's poem, "Green, how I love you, green," was written long before, but his invocation to the color came back to both of them as they rode. This landscape was as green as Galicia, much greener than Granada ever is; the shapes were very different.

After an hour and a half the road widened, flattened, before starting up again, and suddenly the lake was there. Cummings stopped the car at the very edge, and pointed along the gravel shore to the family cottage. Not a big house, not a big lake, and rendered smaller to the eye by the green-clad island centered in it. A lake to be loved and held in the mind, a lake to be rowed over, swum in. A lake to be called "*our* lake" and made the source of poems.

The house, built of wood and copper screening, is set on the side of the hill in such a fashion that dwellers climb up steep steps to enter. Mrs. Cummings, gray haired, gentle, had heard the sound of the car, and waited at the top of the steps to greet them. She held out a welcoming hand, and Federico, with a gesture never before seen at Lake Eden, bent with his most courteous Spanish bow and kissed her fingers. She had no words of Spanish, he none of English, but the accord between them was instant. It never wavered. She reminded him of his mother, he said, and her presence soothed his sharp sense of being lost in a strange and potentially inimical world.

A Vermonter, and the daughter of a Vermonter, Addie Cummings knew all the small and universal things of nature that had been the Spaniard's friends from childhood, and the subjects of his earliest poems—the ants, the insects, the lizards, the flowers and the "damp and fragile ferns" that grew in Vermont as in Granada. She knew their ways and so did he; somehow that knowledge bridged the language gap between them and comforted the homesick Spaniard. He would bring her flowers, group them into new combinations and she would welcome them. He could find blackberries—familiar *zarzamoras*—in the fields, and she would make pies and puddings from them.

Most of all she made doughnuts while he waited, straddling a chair with his arms across the back, chin on hands and black eyes sparkling, watching the sputtering fat turn them brown, and when they were out of the fat and laid on brown paper to cool, putting out a finger to test their temperature and then eating, eating, eating.

What else Federico did in Eden, besides establishing a state of mutual affection with an elderly Vermont lady and gorging himself on her doughnuts, is recorded in a memoir which Philip Cummings wrote for his mother, but never published. This report is taken from that memoir of what Federico did, with bits of what he said. The poems that he wrote there, and afterwards, are the shadow under the sunshine. They form a poet's record of how he felt in the landscape of northern Vermont which surrounded him and of how, amid that landscape, he struggled with his own unhappiness and his memories of Spain which, for reasons that must be surmised rather than made clear, haunted and tormented him.

He and Cummings went walking in the woods the morning after his arrival; it was a glorious day, with scarlet and magenta hints of autumn already showing in the branches. The poet's eye, alert since early childhood for the small things of nature, caught rolls of dust in the path, "each one a small world, with its own shadow." Thickets of young dogwood caught at his sleeves, and he declared them "protests of the woodland at the violation of its virginity by our trespassing." He stumbled on a decaying stump, and declared it "the ruin of a Babylonic citadel" (Babylon was repeatedly in his mind these days; as a metaphor it meant to him specifically New York, but his first six weeks in the city so fixed it in his mind that he transferred it even to the spiked and rotting tree). Another stump, so far disintegrated that little remained of it but a wooden skeleton holding a pile of brown powder, brought him to his knees. This, he declared, was once a castle, and he would restore it. Deft brown fingers shaped the castle's keep and the towers, linked them with moss to the standing edges. It was a castle on the horizons of La Mancha, a castle which might have attracted the lance of Don Quixote. It was Federico, playing house in Eden as in Granada.

A moment later, as they scrambled around a barrier in the path, Cummings pushed a rotting tree to the ground. Federico shook his head at this "American cyclops, intent on destroying the weak and the unfit."

Apple trees, old and gnarled, caught his eye, *manazumares,* wild blackberries, *zarzamoras,* the red autumn hips of wild roses, blue asters, towering mullen and yellow goldenrod which he had never seen in Spain. With another dweller in Eden, young Stanton Ruggles, they found a deserted village which, like all abandoned things, caught the poet's eye; its forgotten houses made their way into his Vermont poems. They climbed Mount Morris, and a round hill nearby became for Federico *Las marmacitas.*

Meanwhile Federico worked not only at the creation

of new poems which came beating at his brain, but at analyzing words, in an attempt to help Cummings move older Lorca poems from their native Spanish into alien but equivalent English. Several times that year Federico, who had no skill in any tongue but his own, showed an insistent desire to have his work put into English. To a man as gregarious and vocal as he was the frustration of being surrounded by people who could neither understand nor respond to his poems—which had become the normal crown of his speech—was repeated torture. What he wanted most of all was to be understood, admired, loved. These gifts his poems won for him in Spain. If they were to be withheld in English-speaking America for lack of understanding, then let someone turn his poems into English. That this was a task of great difficulty, requiring a poetic talent almost as great as his own, he hardly recognized.

The kitchen table, near a window facing the lake, was the best working place when Mrs. Cummings was not cooking. Here Federico and Philip sat, hour after hour, with a volume of the second edition of Lorca's *Songs* between them and a pad of paper in front of Cummings, trying to put them into English. Cummings knew Spanish; his vocabulary was adequate both to current and to literary usage. But Federico's handling of words, even in poems written five years earlier, was far from commonplace and it was distinctly literary in his own creative way. He had already, in his "Ode to Salvador Dalí," made his entrance into surrealist phraseology. There were long discussions between the two men about those words and their visible and invisible meanings. In these discussions Federico could only explain, and in Spanish, what he was saying with a phrase that was far from clear. "Each poem was a mental wrestling match," Cummings wrote in his journal. "The translations stand as approved by Federico." But the latter had no basis for judging any English version.

The attempt was honest and earnest, made with the best will in the world on the part of both Federico and his host. This was the first translation made of these poems into English. Only recently published, it is a touching reminder of those days in Eden.

The cabin had no piano, and Federico had come without a guitar. The two men sang familiar folk songs together, but Cummings wanted more than that. He was proud of his guest, and he longed to share the guest's special skills with his Lake Eden neighbors. Language alone would not do it, even for two gentle schoolteachers who lived nearby, loved poetry, but knew no Spanish. Remembering the delight of the poet's music at the *Residencia,* "Felipe" persuaded Federico to sing for the village. The yellow-sided dance hall around the curve of the lake had a piano—not well tuned, but neither was the piano in the Hotel Washington Irving in Granada where he had played more than once. Cummings invited Stanton Ruggles who lived all the year around in Eden village; "The Boy Stanton," invited his friends; so did the two retired schoolteachers, the Misses Tyler who lived further up the road behind their handmade stone wall.

At four in the afternoon the village people came in, shy but curious. In a pattern which came to be repeated again and again in more sophisticated New York rooms Federico told them about the song he was going to sing and Cummings translated what he said into English; it would be the tale of the burro who carried the vinegar for the village (which he had sung at his first meeting with the Chilean Morla Lynch), or the one of the four mule drivers, or any other from the rich storehouse of Federico's memory. For the moment he forgot, as he always did, that his words were foreign to his audience. And by that charismatic miracle of charm, personal evocation, artistry which was his own great gift, he made his audience forget. They had been told what the song would be about—gestures, voice, and that ineffably vivid face conveyed even more than the friendly translator's words. Federico had never in his life failed to hold his audience, and those Vermont farmers in the bare Eden dance hall offered no exception. They cheered, they pounded on the floor, they crowded around to shake his hand. He had won Eden.

He won it, and he left it. August was ending. Ten days in a totally strange atmosphere, with only a single friend (beside the family dog) with whom he could talk, was enough. A letter to Angel del Río is a homesick confession of the desire to get out of the past—the Vermont village past that in essence (and in American terms) was so like the village past of Fuente Vaqueros, or Zajuira, but quieter, green instead of gold, sadder because it was not his own village.

Ten days was enough. It was time for him to go back to the city, to friends of his own tongue.

Before he went away to visit Professors Angel del Río and Federico de Onís in their summer homes in the Catskills, Federico left with Philip Cummings a packet of manuscripts, some thirty pages which he did not want to take to the communal Spanish life at Columbia. He asked Cummings to keep them safe for him, and Cummings did. He kept them safe until after word came of the poet's death. Each year before, on what became almost an annual trip to Spain, he had asked Federico if he should bring them back, and each year Federico said "no—keep them for me." After August 1936, when the news of the poet's assassination reached Cummings, he opened the packet and read the pages. "They were dreadful," he said with that firm closing of the Vermont mouth which means that no further questions will be welcome. "I burned them."

What was "dreadful" in them no one but Philip Cummings will ever know, nor can one say whether they would have seemed as "dreadful" in today's literary light as they did by the stricter standards of 1936. That they revealed the poet's preoccupations seems certain, and that they shed light on the mysterious "crisis sentimental" which spurred him to come to New York. But the question still remains as to what that "crisis" was.

Of what the poet wrote in Eden, we have the classification of his first American translator, the late Rolfe Humphries, who put into English the volume *Poet in New York* in which the Vermont poems are included. Lorca's friend José Bergamín, who published the Spanish edition of that volume in Mexico the same year, used the same grouping. The Vermont poems appear under two headings, "Poems of Lake Eden Mills" ("Poemas de Lago Edem Mills") and "Introduction to Death: Poems of Solitude in Vermont" ("Introducción a la Muerte: Poemas de la Soledad en Vermont"). The first group included two poems, "Double Poem of Lake Eden" ("Poema Doble del Lago Edem") and "Living Heaven" ("Cielo Vivo"). The second has five poems: "Death" ("Muerte"), "Nocturne of Emptiness" ("Nocturno del Hueco"), "Landscape with Two Tombs and an Assyrian Dog" ("Paisaje con Dos Tumbas y un Perro Asirio"), "Ruin" ("Ruina"), and "Moon and Panorama of the Insects" ("Luna y Panorama de los Insectos").

A few of these bear specific dating. "Living Heaven" is dated Eden Mills, Vermont, August 24, 1929. Another poem, "Earth and Moon" ("Tierra y Luna"), not included in these groups, appeared in a Madrid magazine in 1935, and in 1948 was published in Buenos Aires in Diaz-Plaja's study of Federico; this was dated Vermont 1929, "*de la cabaña de Don Kumium.*" This, given Federico's difficulties with English and peculiarities of handwriting, may certainly be translated "from the cabin of Don Cummings." "Ruin," included specifically in the Vermont group, is remembered by Cummings as having been written in the cabin. "Death," the first poem of the group, "Introduction to Death," starts with a poem to Death which is an extraordinary essay in transmigration; it begins:

> What effort!
> Horse into dog,
> Dog into swallow,
> Swallow into bee,
> Bee into horse.

Later, this was to make its way, modified in substance but not in manner of handling, into the Roman Queen scene of his partially published play, *The Public (El Publico).*

On the other hand, Professor del Río claims "Landscape with Two Graves and an Assyrian Dog" for Newburgh. The Newburgh group of poems which begins with "The Boy Stanton" thereby poses a small mystery of its own. Were there two boys called Stanton, one in Eden and one in Newburgh, who attracted Federico's attention? As a first name, Stanton is not a common one, yet there was certainly a Stanton Ruggles of Lake Eden, then aged ten or thereabouts, who went tramping the Vermont hills with Cummings and García Lorca; he grew up to fight and be killed in World War II. Professor del Río, in his study of Lorca, says that a farmer near the Newburgh cabin had two children, a boy and a girl, to whom Lorca was devoted, and assumes (or implies) that one of them was the Stanton of the poem that bears his name. It is, of course, entirely possible that the poet merged the two children, and that what came out was this touching admonition to the lad, "fool and fair among the little animals" whose ignorance "is a mountain of lions," and whom Federico bids to

> Go to learn the heavenly words
> That sleep in the trunks, in clouds, in tortoises,
> In sleeping dogs, in lead, and in the wind
> In lilies that never sleep, in unmocking waters,
> To learn, my son, things your people have
> forgotten.

Such efforts to tie individual poems to the inspiration of individual places are as unproductive as they are tempting. It cannot be repeated too often that Lorca was in no way a literal reporter, nor did lineal thought or photographic memory either attract him or characterize his writing. Yet by the same token, although he wrote about *el Hueco*—the Void—he did not by any means write within a void. As he had told the Madrid audience earlier, "imagination is limited by reality; one cannot imagine what does not exist; one needs objects, landscapes, numbers, planets. . . ." Landscapes, mountains, fern beds, people and moons and water and animals beat upon his consciousness and his subconsciousness, and were transmuted into poetic images by his imaginative genius as the piled dust of a Vermont birch tree was molded by his deft hands into the shape of a Quixotian castle.

His poems of Vermont—written in Vermont or with memories of Vermont shadowing their images—were neither light nor gay nor specifically descriptive of a place where he must have felt himself lonely and alone, however cherished. They were, in essence, poems about himself, his preoccupations, his sorrows and his visions.

Of those sorrows, one can quote from the "Double Poem of Lake Eden" such verses as these:

> Here you drink my blood
> My temper, a child outgrown,
> While my eyes break in the wind
> With the aluminum and voices of the drunkards.

He knew he was "a child outgrown" and he knew this made him trouble. The poem goes on to say,

> I know the most secret uses
> Of an ancient rusty knife
> I know the horror of certain staring eyes
> Over the concrete surface of the plate.
>
> But I seek no world, I sound no voice divine
> I seek my freedom and my human love
> In the darkest corner of the unsought wind
> My human love!

And he wanted a garden. Also he wanted to weep—

> I want to weep because I want to weep
> Like the bad children on the farthest bench
> I am not man nor poet nor even leaf
> But wounded pulse, sounding the other side.
>
> I would weep crying my name
> Rose, child, and silver yew on the shore of this lake
> To tell my truth, as a man of spirit,
> Killing in myself the sneer, the suggestion of the word.

These are not the poems of a happy man. Neither are his very different poems about New York. Both are strange, unhappy, prophetic and at times perverse in their different ways. What distinguishes one group from the other is the surrounding background and its effect on the poet's mind. When he wrote in Eden,

> My archaic voice
> Ignorant of the thick and bitter juices.
> Divined licking my feet
> Under the delicate dampened ferns.

it was the Vermont woodland that infused the words and the images he chose. Those ten days in Eden gave his poetry a dimension that was unique and irreplaceable. For his poems in New York that were to follow, those Vermont poems supplied a balance, a depth of American background that made the latter both more pertinent and more profound. Lovers of Lorca's poetry—and they are scattered across the world from Madrid to Buenos Aires and around the world's other side—owe a debt to the long unidentified American who invited Federico to spend ten August days with him and his parents in the evergreen country in northern Vermont.

Philip Cummings' mother, Addie Cummings, came quickly to love this strange friend of her son whose words she did not know, and Federico, with his quick and instinctive love of the loving, adored her. When he left Eden he wrote to "*Queridísima Señora,*"

> Mother of all mothers, I who am the son of all sons salute you. You have honored me with your smiling attentions. You left me showered with atten-

tions that will endure for all the years to come, for whole centuries of years. I salute you with the affection of the individual being for Mother Earth.

Love me and never forget me.

Your overseas son,
Federico.

8

CHAPTER

New York, and "I'll Go to Santiago"

FEDERICO'S RETURN FROM EDEN WAS as characteristic as his reaction to the green hills, the lakes, the ferns and Mrs. Cummings' doughnuts. After several days in that sympathetic but un-Spanish house he sent off a letter to his friend Professor Angel del Río who was spending the vacation with his family at Shandaken in the Catskill mountains. The letter is the mirror of the homesick man:

> Very dear Angel:
>
> I write you from Eden Mills. Very amusing. It is a prodigious landscape, but of an infinite melancholy.
>
> A good experience for me. I will tell you all about it. Today I only want you to tell me how I can find you so that I can go to you within a few days.
>
> It does not stop raining. This family is very loveable, and full of a soft enchantment, but the woods and the lake put me into a state of poetic desperation which is very hard to bear. I write all day long, and at night I feel exhausted.
>
> Angel; write me by return mail how I can find you. When I think that I can drink in the house where you live it makes me very happy.

Now night is falling. They have lit the oil lamps, and all my childhood comes back to memory in a glory of wheat and poppies. Hidden among the ferns I found a distaff covered with spiders. In the lake not a single frog sings.

Cognac is urgent for my poor heart. Write me, and I will come to find you.

And many greetings to Amelia. Kiss the boy (on his feet) and you will receive an embrace from your friend,

Federico

(Pursued in Eden Mills by the liquor of romanticism.)

And on the other side of the page,

You will tell me how to come. If it is easier for you, send me a long telegram explaining everything.

It would be better for me if you send a telegram.

Anyhow I shall have to come through New York. It is probable that I leave on Thursday. This is a refuge for me, but I am drowning in this mist and this peace which brings forth memories in a way that burns me up,

Addio, mio caro

He was homesick, he longed for his own people, he wanted a drink, which among law-abiding people like Addie Cummings was, in that year of prohibition, unthinkable. His Spanish friends would understand him.

He left by train, as he had come. To get to Shandaken, on the west side of the Hudson River, he must go to New York and out again. This he did successfully, but then trouble caught him. His host Professor del Río, who awaited him, tells the tale of his adventures in the Catskills.

> "Knowing his incapacity for coping with all practical matters I wrote him detailed instructions. He must wire me the time of arrival in Kingston; in case I were not there, he must take a bus to Shandaken. The day we were waiting for him no telegram came and there was no sign of Lorca. We began to be worried lest he might be lost, when at nightfall we saw a taxi chugging along the dirt road of the farm. The driver wore an expression of resigned ferocity, and Federico, half out of the window, on seeing me, began to shout in a mixture of terror and amusement. What had happened, of course, was that Lorca, finding himself alone in Kingston, had decided to take a taxi without being able to give the right directions to the driver. They had been going around mountain roads until a kindly neighbor had given them our address. The fare was $15.00. As Lorca had spent all his money, I had to pay the driver and placate his fury. Federico's terror was the outcome of his conviction that he was lost, without money enough to take care of the bill. Immediately he gave the incident a fantastic twist and said that the driver, whom he could not understand, had tried to rob and kill him in a dark corner of the woods."

After the story had been told, the brandy drunk, the waiting supper eaten, it was revealed that the two months old baby, whose feet Angel had been asked to kiss on Federico's part, was ill with a throat infection. The doctor said the child must not sleep in the mother's room; as Federico had the only guest room, the baby's crib was tucked into the far corner. After a few days the guest protested.

"But why, Federico?" asked the harassed mother. "Does he cry and keep you awake?"

The poet, though in Spain he must have seen a brother and two sisters go through babyhood, shrugged: "I don't sleep. He doesn't move, he doesn't cry, he doesn't do anything. I stay awake watching him. I think he's died." With some difficulty, the poet was persuaded to put up with the baby a day or two longer.

The mother's routine was to give the child a bottle at two in the morning. Early the next morning, bottle in hand, Amelia opened the guest room door without a sound. There was the sleeping baby. There also was the unsleeping poet, sitting on the edge of the bed, watching the silent child. "He doesn't move. He hardly breathes. Are you sure he's alive?" The baby's mother was quite sure.

A few days later the del Río family moved themselves and their guest back to New York, where their apartment became his temporary refuge. He did not stay there. As he had decided not to register at Columbia for another useless period of lessons in English, he moved into an apartment which an ancient address book reports was at 542 West 112th Street; there he could look over lower buildings at the Hudson River. He was near the University, but not in it.

The months between September, when Federico came back to New York for the normal winter season, and March (or April), when he went to Cuba at the invitation of the *Institución Hispano-Cubana de Cultura* to deliver four lectures, are frequently pictured by his Spanish friends as lonely, devoid of contact with Americans or literary people, and with the poet saved from despair only by visiting Spaniards. This picture of the poet in New

York is both chauvinistic and inaccurate. Federico had warm and admiring friends among Americans who spoke a certain amount of Spanish; his charms also conquered many who had little or none of that language. He even was said to have won admirers among a group of wealthy Park Avenue fashionables who invited this interesting stranger to elegant parties and used French as a means of communication. Knowing what a thicket of miscomprehension his heavily accented French and their American version must have created between them, one appreciates how much magic his charisma must have exercised.

How he got around New York, with no English, and little sense about the geography of the city, was a continual surprise. He claimed to be able to say "Tim-es Esquare" in four syllables, but nothing else. One day a friend appeared at a Columbia student restaurant and asked Federico in Spanish, "What are you eating?" "I always have ham and eggs" was the answer, "because I don't know how to ask for anything else."

He told another friend that in the subway or the streetcar he had two techniques, one for getting a seat, the other for getting off through a crowd. To get a seat he would pretend to be lame, and out of pity someone would rise to give him a seat. When he left he would stand very straight, then make a bell sound, "talán, talán, talán," and go out swinging his arm in time, as though swinging a censer. As for the American rite of punctuality, he seldom arrived anywhere on time, but his friends knew that Spaniards refused to be slaves to clocks and only new acquaintances would grow worried or angry.

His Spanish friends were many, both in the University where Federico de Onís and Angel del Río ruled the academic kingdom, and outside it where he saw such visitors as Leon Felipe who translated Walt Whitman into Spanish, Gabriel Maroto who was Federico's first publisher (and who explained that the things he thought in Spanish were too valuable for him to waste any time learning English). Also there came Julio Cambo, an amiable Madrid writer both wise and funny, Sanchez Mejías the bullfighter, José Rubio Sacristán, a tall and lively lad who later became Dean of Law at the University of Valladolid, Dámaso Alonso, Argentina, the wonderful dancer, and Argentinita, less classic but always delightful. Columbia University staged an homage to Argentina in Philosophy Hall on December 16th. Federico read from his "Poem of Deep Song" ("Poema del Canto Jondo"), and a memorial pamphlet was issued. The previous month he wrote Morla Lynch that he was working hard, and that he had in hand a book of poems and a play. He gave some lectures; the American poet Muriel Rukeyser remembers that he was invited to present his lecture on "*Las nanas infantiles*" at Vassar.

His Spanish friends took him to Harlem, to Coney Island, to the Battery to see Brooklyn Bridge and across it to see Hart Crane. Angel del Río describes some of his reactions to the city.

"The most extraordinary thing was to wander with him through those streets of the 'melting pot,' the lower East Side and Harlem, full of strange life, a mixture of Dantesque inferno and of *feria* pushcarts where the most primitive and elemental people come from the five parts of the world, live in a monstrous state of anachronism beside the products of a society that is mechanical and bent toward the future.

"At times another great poet, Leon Felipe, another singer of the Spanish people in their deepest desire for justice, went with us. He was a completely opposite temperament. A serious and absorbed Castilian, always in control of himself. For that very reason he loved—with an almost paternal weakness—the abundant and generous vitality of Lorca who moved in these wanderings like one astonished."

His (Lorca's) favorite phrase was "I don't understand anything." He said it shouting, with great expressive gestures in the middle of the street, crowning all this with a great roar of laughter. He understood it. He understood everything. All the images, apparently unconnected, in his then unpublished poems about New York "were the sensations registered in the poet's imagination by the truly chaotic confusion which to us, deprived of the divining authority of the poet, appeared so natural and so common . . ." (this was 1929–1930—the poems did not appear in book form until 1940).

One night del Río took Lorca to see the canyons of Wall Street, impressive under a full moon. This was the period of the great economic crash, when the newspapers were full of the catastrophic fall of prices and the tragic suicides of ruined men. Federico's first reaction was a shout, "I see it, I understand it now. How wonderful!" His second took the form of poetry, including perhaps the most startling poem ever written about Wall Street in any era. Called "Dance of Death" ("Danza de la Muerte"), an early stanza warns of

> The Mask! Behold the Mask!
> Sand, crocodile, terror over New York.
> Profiles of plaster prisoned in an empty sky,
> Ringing with voices of those who die in the
>   droppings of corruption.
> A sky pruned and pure, identical with itself,
> with the first growth and sharp iris of invisible
>   mountains.

The poem, after celebrating the prophesied modern dance of death, ends thus:

Soon, soon the cobra will hiss in the upper stories

The nettle burst through terrace and patio
The Stock Exchange be a pyramid of moss,
The jungle vines come writhing after the rifles
And soon, so soon, so soon!
Alas, poor Wall Street!

The meeting with the young Hart Crane was less fruitful. The friend who took Federico to Brooklyn to meet the American described it with some hesitation. Crane, whose homosexual tendencies were hardly secret, was at the time surrounded with young sailors. Illegal beer ran freely. All of them were drunk. It was not an ideal moment for an American poet and a Spanish poet to forge a friendship. There was even doubt that the American had comprehended who the Spaniard was.

Afterward, Lorca wrote his "Unsleeping City, a Brooklyn Bridge Nocturne" ("Ciudad sin Sueño, Nocturno del Brooklyn Bridge"), which begins,

No one under heaven is sleeping. No one, no one
at all.
The moon's creatures creep sniffing the cabins,
Live iguanas will come to bite the unsleeping men
And he who flees with broken heart will meet at
the corners
The incredible crocodile quiet under the tender
protest of the stars.

Anybody who has ever crossed Brooklyn Bridge and seen the wide Manhattan pattern of lights at any hour of the night will recognize the vivid impression of a city that does not sleep. The iguana and the crocodile, tropic beasts, are harder to relate to reality, but he mentioned them so frequently in his New York poems that one can only think them his preferred images of horror.

It was not that he did not know the seasonal irrelevance of tropic images to the New York scene, did not know the city in a winter snow. In a Christmas poem he wrote that

> Manhattan snow weighs down advertisements
> And takes, through the false arches, purer grace
> While idiot priest and feathered cherubs go
> Following Luther along their lofty ways.

Federico's American friends were necessarily somewhat selective in presenting the poet to other people. It was not always easy to entertain a guest who spoke no English, even when his charm was such as to win most hearts on sight. The tongue and the ears were less flexible than the eyes, and Spanish was a language less familiar to New York ears then than it has been since hundreds of Puerto Ricans began arriving. Herschel Brickell, a tall publisher who loved Spain and Spanish (he later became a diplomat in Latin America), and his wife Norma, a musician as beautiful as a Renaissance Madonna (and more than a bit fey), were always generous in calling in people to meet Federico who might interest him. Not many of them did, but the Brickell apartment on Park Avenue became an American home where he could drop in at will. So, with somewhat less success, did the apartment of Ray and Gertrude Brown, respectively artist and musician.

These latter had been in Granada; they were warm and friendly people; they cherished a grand piano in the living room. Federico went from time to time to play and sing for them, always with a friend to translate the substance of his folk songs. Ray Brown, a man of boundless generosity, had a theory that foreigners who came to America liked to meet each other. He was the guiding spirit in a group of struggling immigrant boys who belonged to the Boys Club at 10th Street and Avenue A, and he thought it would be mutually enjoyable for the poet and the boys to take Federico there where he could sing for them. Alas, Federico was not interested. The idea failed to catch his imagination, left him cold, and the project came to nothing.

The most memorable meeting began with a dinner at the Brickells' on Christmas Eve, followed by a midnight mass. There were only five friends on hand—Herschel and Norma, Federico, the present writer, and a young Englishman named Jack Leacock who, having been born and brought up on the island of Madeira, spoke Portuguese and could make a stab at Spanish. Surrounded by people who loved and understood him, Federico was in splendid form. He had done a great deal of work since he arrived in June, and he hungered for a chance to try it on this audience. Particularly, he had finished *The Love of Don Perlimplín with Belisa in the Garden.* The Brickell apartment included a curving window that opened toward the East River. There Federico sat enthroned, with the rest of us grouped to listen. As a reader he was also an actor, making the play move with his voice. This was the first recorded reading of *Don Perlimplín.* It was not played until 1933, but all four listeners saw it in imagination that night. So enthusiastic were we that Federico insisted on giving me the script to translate into English. I did, but . . .

Shortly after eleven o'clock the party, full of good food, good drink, good enthusiasm, put on hats and coats and struggled out to find a taxi in the snow. Only Federico was Catholic, but everybody knew how important is midnight mass—*La Misa del Gallo* (cock's mass) is what Spaniards call it—and we had been told that the best music could be found in a Jesuit church on the west side of town.

We arrived at the address, still intoxicated with the romantic beauty and wistful allegory of the play, and pushed our way into the crowded church. Jack Leacock was an English Episcopalian; the others were assorted Protestants. From the point of view of religion, only Federico could feel entirely at home in the glory and pomp of the service. And this he did, with praises for this evidence of Catholicism in "Babylonic" New York which, in view of his declared anti-clericalism, were surprising.

The church was hung with Christmas garlands, the music was old and beautiful. But the sermon, being full of praise for progress and expansion, might have doubled for a speech before the Chamber of Commerce. Fortunately it was lost on Federico. The priest's voice was rich and fruity; his message was carried by loudspeakers to the very back of the church where we stood. In those days loudspeakers were a rarity in Spain, and Federico, in the Granada Cathedral, was used to hearing only a thin priestly mumble. Standing, crowded, the party stayed for half the long mass. When we went out into the cold it was amid Federico's emphatic cries of "*Qué maravilla! Qué misa más preciosa. No he visto en España una Misa del Gallo tan hermosa.*" ("What a beautiful mass! I never saw so beautiful a midnight mass in Spain!") The rest said quietly to each other, "Nice music. But what luck that he couldn't understand that awful sermon!"

Some of the parties given for him were not as successful. A woman's club, distinguished for its devotion to literature and other arts, gave a dinner in his honor where he shared attention with a singer of American folk songs named Jack Niles. Folk music was supposed to be a bond between them. Both of them sang for their supper, both were applauded, neither understood the other's language.

Had Federico sung in French he would have been understood. As it was, the audience cheered for his charm; and as he departed the limp that always signaled fatigue showed in his walk.

Along with language difficulties, an obvious point of unhappiness for him lay in the Volstead Act. Liquor in Spain was a recognized accompaniment of life. Liquor in the United States was at that time forbidden by law, although in New York it was widely obtained illegally. The literary world as a whole paid little heed to the prohibition act. People with less money to spend bought drinks less bearable, and the physical effects were worse. Federico saw these under Brooklyn Bridge and at Coney Island, and wrote about them.

In spite of his insistence to del Río that his "poor heart" needed whiskey, Federico was not, in those days, an insistent drinker, nor was he willing to gulp anything reputed to be alcoholic no matter how bad it tasted. It was Scotch whiskey which was just becoming fashionable in Madrid among the young café loungers, but Federico in New York seemed to prefer beer (weak beer limited to a 2 per cent alcoholic content could be bought openly), dry Spanish sherry (of which a few people had been able to buy small quantities from bootleggers), or brandy. Drinking was to him a social accompaniment to conversation, not a governing vice.

The result was that at literary parties in New York, where Americans swarmed and Federico was a treasured guest, he would often be seen with a look of active distaste on his face as he watched the hilarity that flared after cocktails made of "bathtub gin" and canned grapefruit juice. This uproarious laughter, these flushed faces, the indiscriminate pawing between male and female that resulted in certain circles did not happen in polite Spanish society. There was a Spanish word, *juerga,* for parties that might act like this, but they were mostly masculine affairs and young women of good family in Spain did not attend them. Victoria's granddaughter still reigned there in person and in custom, and in manners, at least, Federico was her subject. He might carouse with his men friends in Madrid, he, Dalí and their friends might create Dalian scandals in the streets, he might sing and play all night in Granada's gypsy quarters, but his manners with people like his sisters and their friends continued to be those his mother taught him.

The work he did in New York included the poems that would make his posthumous book *Poet in New York,* a number of individual poems, and two plays, *Don Perlimplín* and a folk play laid in Granada—*The Shoemaker's Prodigious Wife.* He also wrote at least one film script, *Trip to the Moon (Viaje a la Luna)* which was conceived and mostly written in the studio of a Mexican graphic artist named Amilio Amaro. This followed a discussion of the movie *Chien Andalou* by Federico's old friend of *Residencia* days, Luís Buñuel, but it was not then completed on film.

Analysis of the portion of his work written in the United States has been done by people skilled in the art, practice and theory of poetry. There is, however, one observation that should be made for the sake of those who see poetry as the expression of pure genius arising out of the spirit or the imagination of the poet, and bearing no relation to the outward surroundings or experiences of the poet. Of Federico such a statement is demonstrably false. Some of his poems may be hard for an American to understand, his figures of speech far from the actuality that inspired them and hard to relate to it, but the connections between his poetry and his life are surprisingly clear.

Wall Street, Harlem, Brooklyn Bridge, the Chrysler Building, Riverside Drive, the small Jewish Cemetery—

all subjects for Lorca poems—still exist to remind his readers of what he wrote about them. The "Landscape of the Vomiting Multitude" ("Paisaje de la Multitud que Vomita"), a poem about Coney Island crowds at sunset, was an exaggeration of the effect of the alcoholic drinks sold in those prohibition days to people not able to afford to deal with reliable bootleggers whose drinks were easier on the digestion. It is not a pleasant poem, but neither was the reality. In essence this is a form of poetic reporting.

> Murmurs rose from the forest of vomit
> With the idle women, children of burning wax,
> Fermented trees, and never-tiring waiters
> To serve dishes of salt under saliva harps
> No remedy, my son! Throw up,—no remedy.
> Not vomit of the hussar over the harlot's breast,
> Not vomit of the cat that swallowed a frog in a fit
> of absent-mindedness
> They are the dead who scratch with earthen
> hands
> The gates of flint where cloud and dessert are
> rotting.
>
> But the fat woman kept ahead
> And the people looked for drugstores
> Where tropical bitters are set
> Only when the flag went up and the first dogs
> came
> The whole city rushed to the railings of the ferry.

As for "Night at Battery Place" ("Nocturno de Battery Place") and the "Landscape of the Urinating Multitude" ("Paisaje de la Multitud que Orina"), the place, the moon and the multitude are still there in the hot summer, though the "transatlanticos" and their whistles have largely been replaced by the airplanes and their engine roar.

Perhaps for the very reason of their shock potential, some of these poems may arouse the slight aftermath of self-protective humor that sometimes comes with an excess of horror. Not funny at all, but gloomy and poignant, is the poem entitled "Dawn" ("La Aurora") which sits in the section entitled "Poems of Solitude in Columbia University" ("Poemas de la Soledad en Columbia University"). This is the way it looked to Lorca in the summer of 1929:

> Dawn in New York contains
> Four columns of mire,
> A hurricane of dark doves
> Dabbling in rotten water.
> Dawn in New York goes wailing
> Over tremendous stairs
> Seeking among the awns
> Spikenard of painted pain.
> Dawn comes, no one receives it in his mouth,
> For here no morning or hope is possible:
> Sometimes the coins in furious angry swarms
> Sting, pierce, devour abandoned children.
> The first to go out realize in their bones
> No Paradise ever, no loves bereft of leaves;
> They know they go to a heaven of law and
>   number,
> Games without skill, sweat without reward.
> Light is buried among the links of noise
> In a shameless challenge of unrooted science.
> In the wards are people, staggering and sleepless,
> Like late survivors of a bloody shipwreck.

For all the strength and desolation apparent in observations and images like these, it is the poems about Harlem and the Negroes which are most startling in their prescience and their pity. The years 1929–30 when Federico visited New York were notable for the sudden popularity of certain Harlem cafés among what one might call the "intellectual smart set." Carl Van Vechten wrote glowingly about them, interested professors from Columbia and curious fashionables from Park Avenue went to dance or to watch the dancing. It was a period when urban America was discovering Negro music, Negro acting, Negro artistry.

Federico went with Spanish friends, or with the Negro novelist Chester Himes, more than once, and delighted in the music, but his vision soared far beyond that artistry to the whole position of the Negro in American society. It was of this that he wrote with passion and compassionate understanding. He who had seen only an occasional black face in Spain was startled at the number of Negroes in Harlem. He was also startled at the contrast between those blacks who amused the whites for profit in dance cafés and those who celebrated the Catholic Mass in church. He felt the tragedy of the Negro in his low social position, his menial status halfway between doorman and entertainer, with no hope but poverty and despair. What other poets and novelists described in detail much later, this sensitive Andalusian, coming to America for the first time, felt and put into wonderful poetic metaphor forty years ago. The tragedy of being black in a white world has had no greater poetic exposition and protest. In these poems he was truly, as Angel del Río said in 1937, "far from Andalusianism, a poet of a character more universal than the one who wrote 'Ode to the Most Holy Sacrament,' or *Yerma,* a poet with an unsuspected social sense."

The specifically Negro poems are only two in number, "Pattern and Paradise of the Negroes" ("Norma y Paraiso de los Negros") and the deservedly famous "King of Harlem" ("El Rey de Harlem"). These make up in strength for what the group lacks in number. The first might be described as only a trial run of the subject; it is abstract, almost remote, an identification of the Negroes as a people with the same affections felt by Federico himself for field and wind and wave. He finds them hating (as he did) "the punctual farewell handkerchief" but

They love the deserted sky,
Irresolute bovine expressions,
The lying moon of the poles,
The curving dance of the water along the shore.

With knowledge of stem and furrow
They fill the clay with luminous nerves,
Skate wanton over water and sand
Tasting millennial saliva, the bitter freshness.

But it was in "King of Harlem" that this poet touched most deeply the problems and the tragedies of the Negro in that section of New York. This long poem begins with surrealist images that sound as though Federico had just arrived at the door of one of those Harlem cafés which were so popular with black and with white in the late 1920s. He sees the flicker of cigarette lighters, "Eternal fire was sleeping in the flint," and a beetle or two that was "drunk on anise." He sees "That old man, laden with mushrooms" who "went to the place where the black men wept." The café was crowded. He had to make his way through "the little Jewesses that bubble over. For the King of Harlem to chant with his full choir." And then in the deep tones of a *cante jondo* singer he mourns,

Ah Harlem, Harlem, Harlem!
There is no anguish like your oppressed eyes
Your shuddering blood within the dark eclipse,
Your garnet violence, deaf and dumb in the
  shadow,
Your great King prisoner in a janitor's suit.

In one image after another he expresses his horror at the low estate of the black man and his exploitation by the whites. The blood must, he says, somehow find its way out.

The blood is coming, the blood will come
By roof and shed, everywhere
To burn the chlorophyll of the blonde women
To wail at the foot of the bed, before the sleepless
  washstand,
To burst in a dawn, low yellow, tobacco brown.

Take flight! Take flight!
Past the corners, hide in the highest story
For the pith of the forest will penetrate every
  crack
To leave in your flesh the light trace of the
  eclipse,
And a false sadness,—the discolored glove, the
  chemical rose.

The visions and the pity were prophetic to a degree that can only now, after forty years and long revolts against the Negro's inferior status, be recognized. The vision is apocalyptic. With that strange poet's prescience he saw violence coming, and told them,

Negroes, negroes, negroes, negroes
No snake, nor goat, nor mule

Has ever paled at dying.
The woodsman does not know
When the loud trees, cut down, will die.
Wait in the vegetal shadow of your King
Till hemlock, thistle, and the nettle set
And root confusion in the farthest roofs.

And then, at last you can

Beat out assured your dance while bristling
flowers
Murder our Moses in the reeds of heaven.

Federico stayed in New York during the 1929–30 winter season, with its snow and sleet, its spectacular economic crash (about which he wrote his New York poems of tragedy and accusation), its lavish alcoholic parties and its report that hundreds in Tennessee and Oklahoma were suffering from drinking a mixture of Jamaica ginger and creosote, or a crude carbolic acid used as sheep dip. He learned from Madrid that the dictator Primo de Rivera had resigned and been replaced by a general who, strangely, had called Miguel de Unamuno back from exile to resume his university post. He spent hours with the dancer Argentinita, harmonizing Spanish folk songs. He tired of the city, tired of the various forms of death which it imposed on its people and the animals that fed them. His poem entitled "New York" describes

The endless trains of milk,
The endless trains of blood,
The trains of roses, shackled
By dealers in perfumes.
The ducks and the doves and the hogs and the
sheep
Shed their drops of blood

Underneath multiplication
And the terrible outcries of cattle, jammed
together
Fill with grief the valley
Where the Hudson rolls, drunk on oil.

His condemnation of it all was bitter;

I damn all the people
Who ignore the other half
The half beyond salvation
Raising the concrete mountains
Where little forgotten beasts
Know the beat of their hearts,
And where we shall all go down
In the final feast of the drill.

I exorcize the spell
Of those deserted shops
Where agony never shines . . .
Which erase the scheme of the woods,
And I offer myself to be eaten
By the cattle, densely jammed,
Whose outcries fill the valley
Where the Hudson rolls, drunk on oil.

Poet in New York, difficult to translate, came out of season and too early to catch the attention of American critics who later would learn to understand surrealist poetry. The basis of Lorca's prophecy of Negro revolt and his castigation of New York has never been given adequate critical attention. The French were more appreciative and more understanding. Marcelle Auclair, who translated long sections of the New York poems into fine French verse, calls the volume "Federico's Apocalypse" and says that in it the poet condenses the explosive forces that move the world, "love and revolt, love and cupidity, the whole in an obscure desire for eternity." Significantly, perhaps, this collection of New York poems contains the only poetic allusion that Lorca ever made to the first World War, which ended the year that Federico went to Madrid. It is a poem to an "Abandoned Church," and subtitled "Ballad of the Great War." Beginning "I had a son called John" the verses mourn for all sons called John. He was a giant, "but the dead are stronger, and know how to devour pieces of sky."

With the coming of spring, the poet left New York for more sympathetic surroundings. The Hispano-Cuban Culture Institute had invited him to come to Havana and give some of his lectures. He set forth with four manuscripts in his pocket and his memory. He would talk on "Theory and Play of the *Duende*" ("Teoría y Juego del *Duende*"), fashioned out of his love of *cante jondo;* on the old Granada poet Soto de Rojas; on "What a City Sings from November to November" ("Como Canta una Ciudad de Noviembre a Noviembre"); on children's nurses and their cradle songs. All well rehearsed, tried out, proven able to charm audiences.

He went down by boat; the weather warmed as he went; the sky cleared and turned itself and the water blue. Landing at Havana seemed to him a kind of return to Spain and the Spanish-speaking people. Here were Negroes as in Harlem, but here they had added a Latin flavor to their own gaiety. Federico rejoiced openly, cast off his penitential and censorious New York mood, wrote one of his most delicious poems in the rhythm of the Cuban *son*—with the refrain, "*Iré a Santiago.*"

When the full moon comes, I'll go to Santiago de
Cuba
I'll go to Santiago
In a carriage of dark water
I'll go to Santiago

An argument rages as to whether or not he ever went, but certainly he immortalized the town.

He was welcomed by palm trees, by the distorted but familiar Andalusian Spanish that Cubans speak, by a host of friends, would-be friends, and enthusiastic admirers. In New York, despite all that friends could do, he had felt himself basically alone. Here he was once more feted, praised, embraced in his own tongue and with his own gestures. Spiritually as well as physically, he was free of the cold Anglo-Saxon winter and rejoicing in the warm Cuban-Spanish spring. He did little work, but he enjoyed himself abundantly.

He is said to have met everybody, seen everybody, gone everywhere, become, in the Cuban mind, an adored stepson of the island. In spite of that he managed to write some scenes of his surrealist drama, *Thus Let Five Years Pass (Así que Pasen Cinco Años);* he published the prose poem "The Beheading of the Innocents" ("La Degollación de los Innocentes") in a Cuban literary review. There was evidence that in this state of induced euphoria he came to terms with his "defect" and learned to live with it. Also, as Marcelle Auclair comments shrewdly, "because he was happy, freer than a native of Granada had ever dreamed of being," he wrote in Havana, on paper bearing the letterhead of the Union Hotel, his play about all the explosive liberties, *The Public.*

When he left, it was in the company of his friend the distinguished music critic Adolfo Salazar, who had first noted the appearance of his first book of poems with an appreciative review.

Federico came north with Salazar in the summer of 1930. The Spanish critic disembarked in New York and went at once to see Olin Downes of *The New York Times* who was then the city's ruling reviewer of music. The poet stayed on board the ship, out of preference, perhaps, but also out of necessity. His visitor's visa had run out, and he had neglected (or forgotten) to renew it. Forbidden by immigration officers to step on shore, he made telephone calls to Herschel Brickell and other friends, summoning them to a final visit. This turned into a farewell shipboard dinner. Norma Brickell reported the next day what was to be her last sight of the beloved friend. "It's just as well you couldn't come," she said sadly, almost seeming not to believe her own words. "He's not our Federico any more, but a very different person. Wholly male, and very vulgar."

This sea change was Cuba's gift. In Madrid, in 1931, he had shed this and become again "our Federico." Three years later, after his wildly successful journey to Argentina, he wore another and completely different guise.

9

CHAPTER

"Where Is My Play?"

FROM THE TIME THAT FEDERICO got back to Spain in the summer of 1930 until he left for Buenos Aires in the autumn of 1933 he had two chief preoccupations, his impressions of New York and the poems he had written there, and his subsidized travelling theater, *La Barraca.* He also devoted further attention to the play he had read to American friends on the night before Christmas, *The Love of Don Perlimplín with Belisa in the Garden.*

The news that Federico had gone to New York, had there written some "dreadful" poems, and would talk about the city and his poems spread rapidly among his friends. His trip was almost as strange to them as though he had gone to the moon. In those days Spaniards did not commonly travel to North America unless they were Galician workmen, or Basque shepherds going out to tend flocks in Nevada. Paris, yes, Rome, yes, London, perhaps. But not New York.

Federico made good use of his exceptional journey to advance his career. In January 1931 he published four of his New York poems in the *Revista de Occidente.* This recognition delighted his family, but much of the pleasure he got from it took the form of reciting those poems to audiences as jewels of comment in his lectures on New York. In March he gave a reading and recital of his poems on New York in his old center, the *Residencia de Es-*

tudiantes. Some months later he did the same thing for girl students at the *Residencia de Señoritas.* He also read the poems to Ambassador Carlos Morla Lynch of Chile and a group of his friends. He made trips to the north and to the south to read to new audiences. All this was a habit that went back to earlier days, but with the New York poems and lectures on the city the habit took on a new urgency. The need to communicate was always vital to him; now his subject, and his manner of communication, were both new and strange. They must be shared. Also his family must be assured that such travelling was worth while in the economic sense that was his father's foremost measure of success.

New York continued to obsess him, but in his own terms. A year later he gave an interview about the trip to Méndez Domínguez of the Spanish news magazine *Blanco y Negro.* In it he is quoted as falling back on what had even then become a cliché, that "The influence of the United States in the world is counted in terms of skyscrapers, jazz and cocktails. This is all. Nothing more than this." The next observation was less commonplace and more personal. "And they make cocktails better in Cuba where the North American soul thinks it has more power." His own special creation of New York had hardened and taken shape as truth. He had fashioned it not only for audiences in Madrid, but also in Valladolid, San Sebastian and other towns. Later he would present it to Buenos Aires and Montevideo. In the process of trying out the poems he was preparing them for permanent form in print, and hopefully, for wide distribution, processes that his ambition desired while vestiges of his young timidity continued to protest.

Federico professed himself unwilling to describe Madrid or Moscow (there is no record of his having seen the latter city), both of which he thought had been described too often. He said that his observations about New York would be lyrical. In these terms he mentioned New York's "extra-human architecture and furious rhythm, geometry and anguish. Man and machine both live in the slavery of the moment." And then, "snow, rain and clouds emphasize, hide, flood the enormous towers but these, blind to every kind of game, express their cold intent, the enemies of mystery; they cut the streaming lodes of the rain and display their three thousand swords through the swan-whiteness of the fog." And again, "an army of windows, where no single person has time to look at a cloud or to carry on a dialogue with the delicious breezes which the sea keeps sending, but getting no response."

The reporter for *Blanco y Negro* egged the poet on and he responded, "But one must conquer it. One cannot trust lyrical reactions without having rubbed shoulders with people in the avenues and the mass of men from all the world." In the Armenian quarter one night, he had heard a short, vivid description of what had led to a killing. This he made almost immediately into poetry.

> How was it?
> A slash on the cheek.
> That's all.
> A thorn to vex the stalk
> A knife to dive
> To find the roots of the cry.
> And the sea stops moving.
> How was it? How was it?
> So.
> Leave me. Like this?
> Yes.
> The heart alone departed.
> Woe, woe is me!

And he had met others than Negroes—"The races of all the world meet each other in New York; but the Chinese, the Armenians, the Russians, the Germans go on being foreigners. All of them except the Negroes. It is not to be doubted that these exercise an enormous influence in North America; no matter what anyone says they are the most spiritual and delicate element in that world. Because they believe, because they hope, because they sing and because they have an exquisite religious langour which saves them from all their present dangerous anxieties."

At this the reporter expressed surprise. "The blacks?" "Yes," replied the poet emphatically. "The black, not the blonde Americans. What I saw, and wandered in, and dreamed about was the great Negro quarter of Harlem, the most important black city in the world, where the lewdest gesture has an accent of innocence that makes it perturbing and religious and fearful. Negro misgivings everywhere. They fear the rich on Park Avenue." And then, "I wanted to write the poem of the Negro race in North America, and to underline the sorrow which the Negroes feel at being black men in an opposing world; slaves of all the inventions of white men, and all their machines, with the continued fear that some day they will forget to light the gas in the stove, or steer the automobile, or button the starched collar; or they will stick a fork in the eye. Because these inventions are none of theirs. . . .

"Yet what is truly savage and frenzied in New York," he went on, "is not in Harlem. There is human essence there, and childish cries, and there are homes and grass, and sorrow that is consoled and hurts that are gently bandaged.

"But Wall Street is impressive because it is cold and cruel. Gold flows there in rivers from every part of the earth, and death comes with it. Nowhere else in the world does one feel the total absence of the spirit; droves of men who cannot work beyond three P.M. and droves of men who cannot stay beyond six—a despising of pure science and the demoniac strength of the present. A spectacle of suicides, of hysterical men and groups that fall, fainting. A spectacle that is terrible, but without grandeur." And then he remembered the city's effect on his own spirit. "No one can have any idea of the loneliness which a Spaniard feels there, above all a man from the South. Because if you fall, for example, you will be trampled on, and if you fall into the water they will throw down on you the paper plates and napkins from their lunches. The New Yorkers, the multitudes that lean against the bars on the waterfront."

"But the country?" He had seen only Vermont, in August. "A green lake, a landscape full of spruces, a jew's-harp, maple sugar." But in the city, "A military salute for Lincoln. Four blind horses. Songs of the heroic days of Washington. Jasmine. The sky. No struggle between the small town and the cloud, nor do those hives of city windows eat each other up in the dead of night. . . . The sky, like Picasso's terrible big blue mother, runs with open arms along the sea. The country sky triumphs over the skyscrapers."

But now, with a change of pace in his own 1932 present, "New York, at this distance, is fantastic. It becomes as moving as a natural spectacle of mountains or the desert." There was admiration in his tone, but no love. He had never gone back to New York except for the hours that his ship returning from Cuba kept him in New York harbor on his way back to Spain. He thought later that he would go to North America again, but to the Spanish part, to Mexico.

In spite of the fact that Federico's family had moved

from Granada to Madrid when the poet got back from New York, it was with the family of Carlos Morla Lynch that he spent more and more of his time. The moment came when Ambassador Carlos could write in his diary account of Federico that the poet "truly lives in my house, with the good and the bad, the sunny and the sober part of him, as there is everywhere."

On the basis of this friendship that had exploded into being before Federico went to New York, the poet had built a relationship of confidence in which he came to use the Ambassador's apartment as a second home, where no restrictions of any kind kept him from doing or saying exactly what he pleased. The atmosphere there was far freer than it ever had been in his mother's house. Discussions ranged in areas that would have been neither understood nor (if understood) tolerated in Fuente Vaqueros, *Huerta de San Vicente,* or Granada.

The Morla Lynch household was both affectionate and sophisticated. The children were delightful; the Ambassador's wife was beautiful, intelligent and endlessly patient; Federico needed contact with all those characteristics. What the bourgeois provincial poet also got was an accompanying sense of upper class Spanish society that hitherto had never touched him. Discussions with the Chilean Ambassador led to discussions with friendly members of the Spanish nobility. They touched on the fragile monarchy, on the death of a member of the royal family. Federico found himself invited to meet diplomatic society, and while it all suffered from a hint of the *cursi* —the pretentious—there are reasons to believe it made an impression.

In the Morla Lynch family he had an audience that was even more broadly educated and more intellectually appreciative than had been his young friends in the "Little Corner" of Granada who had first opened new worlds to him. Here was a further touch of the international and cosmopolitan aspect of life that he had glimpsed in New York.

The Chilean's own account of his reading to friends, of parties, of Federico's extravagant showing of affection or displeasure sheds a most curious light on him and his family as well as on Federico. Once the friendship between the two was established, everything appeared to have been read to Morla first, everything was discussed, from the dancing of La Argentinita (who Morla thought too refined to do Spanish dancing well) to a projected trip to the Amazon, and the beggars of Madrid, among whom Federico proposed to spend a night. (He never got there.) They all went together to see a private showing of the new Buñuel film, *L'Age d'Or,* which had created a scandal in Paris. Federico, loyal to his old friend, declared the film "full of magnificent things." Morla Lynch was scandalized by its vulgarity, and found it of little value. Federico gave a first reading of *Thus Let Five Years Pass* in the Morla house; he bestowed on his friend Carlos a first edition of his *Six Galician Poems (Seis Poemas Galegos)* and of his puppet play *Don Cristóbal.* He also discussed his evolving plans for a jitney theater, *La Barraca,* which should take classic Spanish plays to the villages of Spain in which no theater had ever existed.

This theater plan was an outcome of the Republican revolution in April 1931 which had banished Alfonso XIII from his throne, taken Madrid with flowers and song rather than with bloodshed, and installed the poet's old friend Don Fernando de los Rios first as Deputy and then as Minister of Education.

What put the jitney theater idea into Federico's head, whether he had heard of such theaters in the United States, or had been inspired by reading of the 16th century Spanish theaters that travelled with a cart and with boards to make the stage—of this there is no proof. He had told me about this dream in the summer of 1931 when I was in Madrid reporting the making of the new Republic's constitution for the Sunday Magazine of *The New York Times,* and I wrote about it.

In 1931 Federico had been one of the first people I saw in Madrid, but by chance rather than by intent. The incident was absurdly characteristic of the man. With a reporter of *The New York Times* who was then stationed in Madrid, I was visiting some of the cafés where politicians and intellectuals met every evening to discuss the day's news, whether it was a political event, a bullfight or the publication of a new book. We were drinking anise, when the *Times* man said suddenly, "Here comes some one to see you." "Impossible, I don't know a soul in Madrid." "Well, it's no friend of mine," he shrugged. "You must know him. Turn around and look." There was Federico coming across the sanded floor, limping a bit, but smiling and looking entirely as he had looked in New York the year before. The "vulgar" Cuban look which had disturbed Norma Brickell was gone. The New York friend was back.

Introductions were made, but Federico refused to sit down, on the grounds that he was with friends. Then, "Where is my play?" he demanded. "In my suitcase," was the reply, given with as little explanation as his question.

"Good. Then I won't have to rewrite it. They're going to put it on," he said, and with no more talk except to ask where I was staying, he returned to his table.

"My play" was, of course, *Don Perlimplín,* which he had left for translation on that magic December night a year earlier when he had read it at the Brickells'. The process of translation had proved impossible. In Spanish the play was delightful; in English it did not make theater sense. Also there was too much poetry in it for a journalist to cope with, particularly one who has always held to the belief that poetry can be translated properly only by a poet. Baffled, I had brought the play back to Spain, expecting to have to search out its author in Granada. That he should be in Madrid, in that café, was as unforeseen as it was welcome.

The rest of the story was not so gay. The play, which had been slated for production before the fall of Primo de Rivera, had been forbidden by the censor on moral grounds. Gossip said that the truth was that the situation of the aging General, who was then proposing to marry a wealthy widow, was too reminiscent of the situation of *Don Perlimplín* to allow witticisms at the General's expense. It had to wait until the arrival of the Republic; then the play was put on privately by the *Club Anfistora,* an amateur organization of almost professional standing.

Federico's venture into the world of travelling theater with *La Barraca* was under active discussion at the same time. It was to be, he said, "Spain's newest gesture toward establishing the arts as an active force in the life of the Republic." The name was usually used to denote one of the small thatched houses set in the midst of Valencia's market gardens. But "this *barraca* will be unusually versatile, taking to wheels and travelling about the countryside, setting up its house in the squares and market places of towns and villages."

The plan was evolved by Federico and his student friends, undoubtedly in a Madrid café, with "blue smoke blurring the lights, a group of students around a marble table littered with tall glasses of *café con leche,* all talking together until the conversation gradually focussed on the theater, the thing García Lorca was saying about it, the possibility of having one of their own." Federico proposed the plan to his friend, Don Fernando de los Rios, then a deputy, who in turn presented it to Marcelino Domingo, then Minister of Public Instruction (a post to which Don Fernando later succeeded). The plan, with a suggested budget of 300,000 pesetas, was presented formally to the Cortes in October 1931 by the *Union Federal de Estudiantes Hispánieos;* Don Fernando argued for it and the Cortes adopted it.

Costs would be limited to needed materials. All the actors would be unpaid students, or friends of the idea working without pay. The project would center first in Madrid, then spread to university centers such as Granada, Salamanca, and so on.

As Federico explained it, "*La Barraca* will really be two *barracas,* one permanent in Madrid, placed preferably in a public park, where plays will be presented while the students are at work in the winter time; the other, the wandering *barraca,* the caravan theater, will go on wheels through the outskirts of Madrid and into La Mancha on weekends and holidays. And in the summer we will tour Spain. We will have an omnibus for the actors, and a truck with two tents, one for men and one for women. That will also carry the scenery. Students will do all the work—students in architecture will make the *barracas* and go along with us in the caravan to do the stage setting and the assembling; students in philosophy will collaborate with the group of poets on the executive committee.

"I myself will be writing new things and helping with the old ones. So will Vicente Aleixandre, our critic, all serenity and sense of balance. So will Manolo Altolaguirre, the angel of *La Barraca,* who is going to the Amazon to write a poem. And Luis Cernuda, and many others." It was Eduardo Ugarte who proved to be *La Barraca's* practical right hand.

In the minds of Fernando de los Rios and the Cortes, the reasons justifying such a new theater were primarily educational. "The theater used to be the most important means of popular instruction, popular exchange of ideas," Federico explained. "In the days of Lope de Rueda (16th century) it was just such a theater on wheels as we are planning now. It went into all the villages, and gave all the famous old plays which foreigners find so marvelous, and which are so badly neglected in Spain. Outside of Madrid today the theater, which is in its very essence a part of the life of the people, is almost dead, and the people suffer accordingly, as they would if they had lost two eyes, or ears, or a sense of taste. We are going to give it back to them in the terms in which they used to know it, with the very plays they used to love. We are also going to give them new plays, plays of today, done in the modern manner, explained ahead of time very simply, and presented with that extreme simplification which will be necessary for the success of our plan and which makes the experimental theater so interesting.

"We are going to try all sorts of things at first, and gradually work out the type and the technique that wins the best response. For instance, we want to put on Lope's famous *El mágico prodigioso* in two days, on two succeeding nights—the first time the old-fashioned, realistic version, the second simplified, stylized, as new as the latest experiment and as old as the most ancient techniques of stage setting and gesture. We will watch to see which the audience prefers."

At times the poet-playwright grew surprisingly practical in his explanation. "We plan to adjust prices to the audience too, to hold invitation performances for the rich people of a town, and then the following night charge little or nothing, so that the working people can come. You see we really are very much in earnest. We believe we can do our part toward the great ideal of educating the people of our beloved Republic by means of restoring to them their own theater. We will take Good and Evil, God and Faith into the towns of Spain again, stop our caravan, and set them to play their parts in the old Roman theater in Madrid, in the Alhambra, in those plazas that see markets and bullfights, that are marked by a lantern or a cross. We have had the dream for a long time, and now we are working to make it come true."

It was a wonderful idealistic plan and it provided fine theatrical experience for the producers (of whom Federico was one) and the players, most of whom were university students. Thanks to Don Fernando and the Republican government the dream came true; the money was appropriated, the student actors and stage hands were enlisted, the theater camions were built.

Once *La Barraca* got its season under way (their first program of plays was presented at Burgo de Osma in Castile, fifty kilometers out of Soria, on July 10, 1932) Federico went back to his refuge on the family farm at the *Huerta de San Vicente,* and there began to write *Blood Wedding.* By the middle of September he was far enough along to give the play a first reading in the Morla Lynch house in Madrid. A week later *La Barraca* under his direction gave Calderón's famous *La Vida es Sueño* as part of the 400th year birthday celebration of the University of Madrid. In December he read his controversial *Poet in New York* to an audience in Barcelona; that same month he saw Cocteau's play *Blood of a Poet,* which, in the minds of some of his friends, spurred him to write *Thus Let Five Years Pass.* The calendar of his achievements, which shows him reading that play in October 1931, does not support this dependence on Cocteau, but the legend stands.

How much *La Barraca* educated the villagers of Spain's old stone and plaster villages, how much it lightened their hard-working and largely arid lives, there is no known measure. One unexpected by-product came later to New York in the form of a series of excellent presentations of Spanish plays which were put on after the end of the Spanish Civil War by professors and students of the Spanish Department at Barnard College. Several of those people had played in *La Barraca,* and the spirit and experience gained there gave their productions in New York a remarkably professional air.

In Spain, *La Barraca* quickly became legendary, but in reality the jitney theater soon underwent the fate destined for most projects having a political subsidy. As political conservatives in the new Republic pushed out liberals, its student members were accused of having moved politically to the left; during the so-called "Black Biennium" which began with rightist elections in 1934, this situation suffered political "correction"—rightists took control. Meanwhile Federico himself had gone to Buenos Aires in 1933 to stay for months, and while he had left his most able friend Eduardo Ugarte to manage matters, the 1934 elections finished the inevitable process of disintegration. The experiment had started with a rousing success, but there was in it no hope for a long life.

In the pleasant years before the 1934 elections the liberal temper of the Spanish Republic that had come to power was giving more scope for the production of plays that had been frowned on by the dictatorship. *Blood Wedding* opened in March in the *Teatro Beatriz* of Madrid, played by the company of Josefina Ortigas. In that instance the time between finishing the play and seeing it on the stage was short. The author had read it to friends in the Morla Lynch apartment on September 17, 1932. Six months later it was on the stage. The theater was full. The intellectual world of Madrid was in attendance—Juanito Benavente with his pointed beard, the Quintero brothers (their comedies a bit out of date but still lively), old friends like Jorge Guillén, the red-headed Pedro Salinas, Moreno Villa of the *Residencia.*

The play won its audience in the tense first act. The

house broke into wild applause and cries of "Author, author." Federico came out pale, trembling, uncombed; disconcerted by this storm of applause, he made only half a bow. The plot went on with the wedding predestined to fail, the bride stolen with her own consent, the inevitable tragedy, the desolate mother, with her broken insistence on the "knife, the little knife" that had taken the life of her only son.

Blood Wedding was the first of the poet's plays to win enthusiastic audience applause in Madrid. This, after the catastrophe of the too early *The Butterfly's Evil Spell* and the cool reception accorded his historical romance *Mariana Pineda,* was a long-awaited victory. Not only did it soothe Federico's ambitious soul, bring him theatrical fame, delight his friends, but it also brought him a financial success which for the first time rendered him independent of his family. At the age of thirty-five he was finally a success in terms that his father would recognize. No longer did he appear as a wayward and frivolous son who wasted his time on poetry and had to be given 150 dollars expense money in order to live for six weeks in New York. Now he was making money, real money that even a wealthy landowner could admire.

Moreover this success generated other successes. A month later the *Love of Don Perlimplín with Belisa in the Garden,* which the Spanish dictator, General Primo de Rivera, had banned, was allowed to be played at the famous *Teatro de España* in Madrid by the *Club Teatral de Cultura* which had taken the place of the earlier *Club Anfistora.* Federico, a newly famous dramatist, in the journalist sense of the phrase, was interviewed by a reporter of Madrid's leading newspaper, *El Sol.* This understandably pleased the *Club Teatral de Cultura,* especially when Federico said there should be many more theater clubs in Spain, because they put on plays that the commercial theater would not accept. He praised the "great animator of all this, Doña Pura Maortua de Ucelay" (whose daughter Margarita now teaches at Barnard College). Of his play, he claimed that Don Perlimplín was the "least cuckolded man in the world. His slumbering imagination awakes with his wife's tremendous deceit; but then he makes all the women in the world cuckolded." The grotesque and the lyric are contrasted; the work is held together by music, with Scarlatti's sonatinas entertaining the spirit through the intermissions. The play is a romantic farce, pretty, highly perfumed, and with a note of sardonic tragedy at the end. No such violent storm of praise greeted it as had welcomed the more conventionally dramatic *Blood Wedding,* but neither was its subtle message refused by the audience. Again, the poet-dramatist's star rode high. He had become in truth Spain's leading dramatist.

A month later Federico confided to Morla Lynch his plans for another romantic tragedy of a very different type, *Yerma.*

Meanwhile he kept on speaking, developing ideas, and writing. In May 1931 his "Poem of Deep Song" was published. Later that year he was busy writing "El Diván del Tamarit." (The University of Granada published it in 1936.) Early in 1932 he was working on his puppet drama or group of plays, *Puppets of Cachiporra,* which Margarita Xirgu and her company planned to put on, with the aid of the dancer La Argentinita. This was a dream never realized.

Carlos Morla Lynch, who among the friends of Lorca played so large a part in those years, details two conversations in which Lorca took part that shed light on his ideas as they appear in some of his plays. One of these concerned women, toward whom his plays show an extraordinary sensitivity; the other had to do with life after death.

About women, the question under discussion was the old one as to whether there could be friendship between men and women which would be purely spiritual ("Platonic" was the term then used in the United States) and psychologically satisfying. Federico's somewhat cynical position was that "A woman can, to start with, demand that this friendship (which I would call affinity) be maintained on a basis of comradeship devoid of any spirit of conquest, but if the man fulfills his promise with no signs of weakening, it will be the woman who shows signs of being offended."

On another evening the discussion turned on phases of the gap between faith and science. One of the guests declared roundly that he believed in nothing that could not be explained scientifically. As the company again showed itself far from unanimous, Federico (who, according to Morla Lynch, was especially admirable when he managed to unite philosophy and grace) took the floor. "A fly," said he, "has his own limits, the limits assigned to a fly. This does not mean that what he is incapable of perceiving, has no existence. The same thing is true of men." But what about eternal continuity? Does man with his soul, and the fly with his, come to an end with death? Federico shrugged, "Man ceases to think and to feel 'here,' because the instrument which allows him to express himself humanly ceases to exist." This, to Morla Lynch, came close to a belief in immortality.

10

CHAPTER

Triumph in Buenos Aires

COUNTRY BOY AS HE WAS at birth and as he always liked to believe himself, it was the succession of three cities on three continents—Madrid, New York and Buenos Aires—that spurred Lorca's development and gave him fame. The first took him, in late adolescence, out of the familiar family nest and family values into the complicated metropolitan world of adult fame and theater. The second extended his experience and his sympathies to a trans-Atlantic world that was new and alien, painful and inspiring. The third brought him international fame on a third continent and in his own tongue.

The measure of his progress is visible in both publications and plays. When in 1918, at the age of twenty, he took the first outward step from his family cradle in Granada to the adolescent haven of the *Residencia* he had published only a youthful book of travel sketches—*Impressions and Landscapes* which, though showing a certain prophetic skill with words, provided few clues to his future work. By the time he reached Buenos Aires in 1933 he had developed into a poet of recognized international stature with two volumes to his credit; in addition, and from his family's point of view more importantly, he had become a trained and experienced theater man with half a dozen plays presented of which the last, *Blood Wedding,* enjoyed a vigorous success. Thirty-five years old, he still kept the amazing *brio* of his adolescent charms. People fell in love with him on sight, and few of them forgot him.

If the New York trip was an unpremeditated attempt on the part of his family to rescue him from his own despair (in 1928 he had written to Sebastian Gasch: "I am very beaten and torn by passions which I must conquer") and from some unsavory rumors that pursued him, the voyage to Buenos Aires was his own joyful response to the theatrical eminence brought him by the success of *Blood Wedding.*

Not only did Madrid audiences flock to see the new play, but so did audiences half a world away in Buenos Aires. There Lola Membrives, an enterprising actress born in Argentina of Spanish parents (her father had been a hairdresser in Cadiz), able to sing as well as to act, made a place for herself in the theatrical worlds of Madrid and Buenos Aires. Spurred by the Madrid success of the new Lorca play, she determined to take it to Argentina. There it opened in the *Teatro Maipu* of Buenos Aires on July 29th, four months after it had become a hit in Madrid. Hailed by *La Prensa* as "a play having outstanding values . . . ," and by *La Nación* as breathing "strong and virile poetry," it proved so popular that Lola Membrives, who played the mother, succeeded in having its run extended and in persuading Federico that he must come in person to witness its great success. The Buenos Aires Society of the Friends of Art helped by inviting him to lecture in that city.

It cannot have been easy to persuade the poet-dramatist to take an ocean trip of that length. He had repeatedly shown distress about the ocean—in Malaga, in Figueras, in New York. In those pre-airplane days, to reach Buenos Aires he had to spend not ten days on the sea, as in going to New York, but three weeks. Yet the lure of being a further witness of his own fame in a distant country that spoke his own tongue was strong. In addition, the trip would improve his own fortune and increase his own fame. He decided that the promised prize was too great to miss. In October 1933 he left Barcelona on the great white Conte Grande of the Italian Line with his friend the scenic designer, Fontanals, as companion. The latter had already mounted some of Federico's plays and hoped to do more in Buenos Aires.

Buenos Aires in those days was still the shining capital of the legendary Spanish South America. Wealthy and conservative, its lines of cultural interest reached toward Europe and its audiences were more interested in European plays that in any written in North or South America. No Perón had yet upset its economic pattern; the political interest of its numerous Italian immigrants in fascist ideas was slight. However, they did pay homage to cultural interests. Federico's arrival was preceded in September by that of the more internationally famous Italian playwright, Luigi Pirandello, who came to attend the world-wide premiere of his play *When One Is Somebody (Cuando se es Alguién).* His companion, Dr. Maximo Bontempelli, was mobbed by a riotous crowd which cut electric light wires at his lecture and shouted "Down with Fascism."

Federico, coming from the still safe Spanish Republic, suffered no such negative violence. He arrived in his true character as poet and playwright. Neither his plays, his lectures, nor the friendships he made carried the least hint of political propagandizing. Even before he landed, the newspapers hailed his coming with pride. *La Prensa* called him "one of the most valuable writers in the modern Spanish world, a personality with many facets, tireless in the cause of art, moving from music and song to the subtleties of theater and of literature, one of the great hopes of contemporary literature in the Spanish tongue." He felt the warmth of welcome early. When the Conte

Grande stopped in Rio de Janeiro, a cable of greeting was handed to him from seven of the best known Argentine intellectuals, plus the Chilean poet Pablo Neruda. When, on October 3rd, the ship was warped into her Buenos Aires landing dock, reporters swarming to meet him found him almost speechless in the face of the turbulent welcome surging about him.

He gave the usual interviews that were demanded, and said the usual things. One newsman reported that he had "entered Buenos Aires like a sirocco, and made out of the whole town an unforgettable fiesta." Another, asking what Federico would look for in Buenos Aires, was told somewhat flatly; "The only thing that interests me is to amuse myself, to come and go, to stroll about, to live. The least of my worries is literature. I never intend to do it, but at certain moments I feel the irresistible desire to write and then, when I produce, I do it with pleasure, without surcease, without resting, in order then to return to my earlier existence." This was Federico's Madrid affectation.

Two unexpected family touches restored his personal warmth and sent him in memory back to Granada. The gang plank had barely touched the dock when a middle-aged couple made their way through the crowds of welcoming strangers. The woman was almost weeping with joy, the man waving his hands in pure emotion. They were his Uncle Francisco, his Aunt Maria, who had helped to bring him up in their town near Granada.

A few weeks later another family touch threw him into deeper nostalgia. A woman came to see him in the theater where one of his plays was being produced, a simple woman who was living in the far outskirts of the great city. At first he did not recognize her, and she only smiled at him, "as one might smile at a memory." Then she said softly, "Federico," and again, "Federico." With this she unwrapped something that was carefully shielded in paper. When she got it clear, she handed him a yellowing photograph of a baby. "You recognize it, Federico?" she asked him.

"No."

"But it is you, yourself. When you were one year old. I saw you born. I was your parents' neighbor. The day you were born, I was going with my husband to a fiesta. I didn't go because your mother was ill. I stayed to help in the house. And you were born. When this photograph was taken you were a year old. You see this break in the paper? Your own little hands made it when the picture was new. You tore it, and this tear in the paper means to me a happy memory of you."

Telling this to a friend, the poet added, "I did not know what to do. I wanted to weep, to hug her, to kiss the portrait, and all I could do was to fix my eyes on the break in the paper. I had made that tear when I was only one year old. And this—my first work, good or bad—was there in front of me. After all, what more could I say?"

Such incidents made this visit very different from the one he had made to North America four years earlier. There he was a stranger, neither family nor reporters met him. In consequence he had found New York "cold and gray" and inhabited by a huge population which knew no word of his language. The dizzying urban giganticism, the tremendous mechanical power, the inexorable eloquence of figures, the unknown tongue—all of that oppressed him, worried him and froze his soul.

Some of the same elements were present in Buenos Aires. The great difference lay in the rapturous personal welcome given him there and in the major language of the two cities. Here people could understand him, and he could understand them. To Lorca, whose realm was made up of words, the difference was as night and day. In Buenos Aires, he was, as Lope de Vega in Spain had been four centuries earlier, a "phoenix of delight." All sorts of people reveled in his presence, not only the intellectuals, artists and amateurs among the Friends of Art who had invited him to come, not only that self-chosen handful of intellectual representatives who had sent that welcoming wire to his ship when it stopped at Rio, but also the vast audiences that flocked to his plays.

His five months there, from October 1933 to March 1934, were busy enough to make a volume in themselves. He continued to be the delight of newspapermen, whose comments sometimes reveal as much about the ordinary life of Buenos Aires in those days as they do of this fantastic Spanish creature whose flights they were privileged to report. No week went by without his engaging in activities that attracted the press. He was going to do something, he did something, he had done something—there was reportable news in every tense. His plays that were put on, the lectures he gave, the receptions that were given him—all were marvels in the proper, huge and sometimes dull town of Buenos Aires that stretched from horizon to horizon, as flat as the pampas and almost as colorless.

The chronology of his visit and his triumphs runs through the city's summer months, from mid-October until March 1934 when he sailed back to Spain. During that southern spring and summer the Spaniard dominated the theatrical life of Buenos Aires. Two companies vied in presenting his plays—*Blood Wedding, Yerma,* the gay *The Shoemaker's Prodigious Wife,* and even his version of Lope de Vega's *La Dama Boba.* All his bag of tricks, including his puppet plays, his poems, his lectures, attracted large audiences. He had the intoxicating experience of holding the culture of the southern capital, thousands of miles away from his native Spain, in the hollow of his hand. The man who had been an unhappy stranger in New York was the feted darling in Buenos Aires.

In the last two weeks of October he gave three lectures, one on his much-quoted "Theory and Play of the *Duende,*" and another on his experiences in New York, illustrated by some of his poems on that city; the third lecture was his "What a City Sings from November to November." A reception was given in his honor; he shared attention with Pablo Neruda at a PEN club dinner, and appeared at a revival of *Blood Wedding* with Lola Membrives and her cast; they had moved from the *Teatro Maipu* to the *Teatro Avenida.* That was the 25th of October, and there the cries of "Author, Author!" were so rapturous and the applause so tumultuous that he made a gay little speech, thanking the audience for the "warmth, cordiality and sympathy with which the beautiful city had received him;" he praised their great river with its welcome to the ships of all nations; he was grateful for that "trembling white dove of confidence which this enormous city has placed in my hands" and he ranged his "small voice" with the great one of the poet Rubén Darío. It was a felicitous speech, and the audience loved it.

November was in public a quiet month, with only two big dinners in his honor. Privately he ranged the city, visited Norah Lange and that determined intellectual Rosa Oliver in her wheel chair, went to San Isidro to call on the famous Argentine literary writer, editor, and literary patroness, Victoria Ocampo, daughter of an old and prosperous Argentine family, young, beautiful and highly intelligent. She had recently started a literary magazine under the combined urging of the American Waldo Frank, the Argentinian novelist Eduardo Mallea, and the Spanish philosopher José Ortega y Gasset. On a rare call from Victoria to Madrid, the philosopher had named the new publication SUR over the long distance telephone.

Victoria had a flair for picking men, and women, of more than ordinary literary merit and making friends of them. She also had two hospitable houses and a fortune that in those pre-Perón days seemed inexhaustible. Federico gravitated naturally to her hospitable welcome. Once there, he took possession of her rosewood piano to fill the rooms with Spanish folk songs and his own gypsy ballads. Her publishing house put out the first edition of his *Gypsy Ballads.*

Another friend, Sara Torme de Rojas Paz (known because of her blonde hair as "La Rubia Rojas Paz"), says that Federico felt "like a fish in good water" in Buenos Aires. One day La Rubia asked him if he would lunch with her alone, because, she complained, he was always surrounded with people more important than she was, and she wanted a chance to talk with him. In her courteous Argentine fashion she went to fetch the poet at his Hotel Castelar, thinking to take him to lunch at the Plaza. His friend the Catalan scenic designer came into the lobby first and then Federico, wearing what was then called his white "monkey suit," a coverall similar to those that garage men wear.

Buenos Aires was then, and is still, a conservative town in matters of dress. People with a social sense did not wear monkey suits when lunching with a lady. But La Rubia, devoted to Federico in any garb, and sure of her ability to prevent any disagreeable incident, introduced him to the Plaza's *maitre d'hotel* as the "famous Spanish poet Federico García Lorca" whom she had brought to taste the best cooking in Buenos Aires. There was no sartorial argument. They lunched in peace and gaiety. Meanwhile the head waiter, with a mixture of pride, policy and news sense, went from table to table explaining to the other guests who this was, and they accepted Federico's peculiar garb as an eccentricity on the part of the great.

Proper dressing had become a matter of amusement with Federico. He, who had taken such highly correct clothes to his first encounter with Madrid, turned careless in his theatrical days; working in *La Barraca,* he habitually wore a "monkey suit," a dark blue one with the symbol of the theatrical company embroidered on his breast pocket. By this time he could laugh at middle class formalities, but when he found that a dinner jacket would be expected of him at his first theater appearance in Buenos Aires, he still had enough sense of tradition to buy the one he had negelected to bring. Ordinarily, moving around the city, he anticipated the fashions of the 1970s, wearing a high-necked pull-over; this casual gesture endeared him to waiters, artists, taxi drivers and others of the non-aristocrats.

Edmundo Guiborg, a newspaper critic who had become one of Federico's fast friends, still remembers the time they came in conflict with the police. It was a Sunday, just before elections. Federico and Guiborg, Eichelbaum, who was one of Argentina's best dramatists, and Pablo Suero had been drinking until a late hour in a café on the *Plaza de Congreso,* a square which is always politically suspect. The closing hour came. The café insisted on shutting its doors; the four young men hunted another. How much noise they were making Guiborg does not remember, but it was enough to catch the ear of the police who were guarding the near-by House of Congress. They took the young intellectuals off to a police station in the Calle Venezuela and questioned them. What did they do? Federico said he was a dramatist. The officer did not believe him. Eichelbaum said he was a dramatist. Official disbelief grew. Pablo Suero claimed to be a journalist and a poet. Guiborg said he was a journalist. Police noses went high in the skeptical air. Finally the officer in charge was persuaded to call the newspaper office of *Crítica* where Guiborg worked, and where someone vouched for his good faith and that of his friends. It took an hour and a half to get them out of the police station.

Somehow, in the midst of all these honors and amusements, Federico managed to find working time. Frustrated with that drama of frustration, he was struggling to finish *Yerma,* and he had gone far enough with it to read the first two acts to a group of friends. He also was working on *Thus Let Five Years Pass* which he did not actually finish until 1936, when the *Club Anfistora* played it in Madrid. Pablo Suero asserts that Federico left the first manuscript of that play with him, but he lost it. Incredible as the gift and the loss seem at this distance, the first at least is in character. With his great abundance of talent, his love of reworking both poems and plays, and his native reluctance to have them put into print, Federico was extraordinarily casual with his manuscript copies. He had left his copy of *Don Perlimplín* in New York when he went back to Spain in 1930. He gave the script of *Poet in New York* to José Bergamín. He left a copy of *The Public* with Martínez Nadal. Thus there is no reason to doubt that he gave a script of *Thus Let Five Years Pass* to Pablo Suero in Buenos Aires. It has not yet turned up.

At a critical moment, Lola Membrives, who was having so little luck with *Mariana Pineda* that she fell ill, announced that she would present the newborn play, *Yerma.* This announcement threw the author into considerable confusion; *Yerma* was still in the embryo state; Lorca had the idea but he had not yet completed the script. A man, even a successful Andalusian poet and dramatist, cannot continuously stay up all night, be prepared for gala lunches and dinners the next day, and find much solid working time in between. Even for a genius the working hours to be captured out of the daily twenty-four are, in such circumstances, limited.

Federico solved his dilemma by taking a boat down

the river to Montevideo at the end of January, and staying there for two weeks in February. The weather was cooler, the friends who were greatly loved but must somehow be avoided if work was to be done, were fewer. True, his presence did not go unnoted. He gave at least three of his famous lectures—the one on the *duende,* the one on Granada, the one on *Poet in New York.* He was entertained by the Ambassador of Spain to Uruguay, who in those Republican days was his old literary friend and admirer from Madrid, Enrique Diez Canedo. But all this merely added spice to his working life—somehow he did get *Yerma* to the point where he could read the first act to an expectant audience in Buenos Aires. He could not, however, finish the third act to his satisfaction, for reasons that Alfredo de la Guardia, writing in 1941 about the author's Buenos Aires visit, recognized. "For that, he needed the country where he was born, from whence he came to Buenos Aires, and where he was going to die," and where the play was laid.

In addition to completing *Yerma* for Lola Membrives, he also got his version of *La Dama Boba* (called *La Niña Boba)* ready for another theatrical star, Eva Franco, and on March 4th, she played it in Buenos Aires. A slightly sour note sounded from those critics who doubted the wisdom of treating a Lope de Vega classic so lightly, but most of them praised the Spaniard's professional skill in cutting the famous 16th century play short and giving it a more modern sense of pace.

Buenos Aires, meanwhile, was beginning to cool in preparation for another winter. Spring beckoned in Spain, and Federico heard the familiar siren call.

Summing up the rewards of this six month visit to Buenos Aires, the critic (and friend) Alfredo de la Guardia points out to what extent the rapturous 1933–34 season forged the Spaniard's great reputation. Up to that time, he says, "not one of his works had gained the solid applause of the Madrid public, enthusiastic but with a limited vision of the theater, and only after the resounding first night of *Blood Wedding* was his stage production judged worthy of his poetry." (It was certainly much more profitable.)

In Buenos Aires in a final interview, Federico told De la Guardia that he had discovered America—not the America of the history of the Spanish conquest, of which he knew little and which seemed to him very dull, but the America of poetry, of theater, of youth.

"Spanish youth," he said, "feels itself more than ever closely united with America. Intellectual curiosity and spiritual eagerness move them toward these American countries. American writers interest us, and we young Spaniards (he was then thirty-six years old) mix well with them, and march at the same pace, shoulder to shoulder, with mutual respect and freedom, like true friends. *Friends,* do you understand? Let us give the word friendship its true, exact meaning."

11

CHAPTER

Conquest of Madrid

FEDERICO AND HIS FRIEND FONTANALS arrived home in April 1934. In Madrid, Lorca found that echoes of his triumph in Buenos Aires had preceded him, but what people most wanted to hear was still his group of poems about New York. He was beset with requests to read excerpts, and to put the whole collection into print. The first he was now willing to do, but not the second. With his old intransigence about committing his poems to the printed page, he could not yet be persuaded to publish those spectacular New York adventures in surrealism.

By June, after having visited with family and friends, he was back in his blue monkey suit, directing his beloved *La Barraca,* though he found it somewhat crippled by the restraints imposed by a more restrictive government than the Republic had been in its first months. Happy and confident with the added theater experience and fame gained in Buenos Aires, he took the jitney theater to Santander, then to Salamanca. But an unexpected tragedy lay in wait for him. In August, in the Manzanares bullring, his beloved bullfighter friend, Ignacio Sánchez Mejías, who, for financial reasons, had gone back to the arena after too many years of absence, paid the penalty of his daring. In a rare reversal of the usual practice, the bout went to the bull. Sánchez Mejías was gored so seriously that he died of the wound. Federico, brokenhearted, turned to poetry to express his sorrow. Many critics consider his *Lament for the Death of a Bullfighter* to be his finest poem. Simple in structure, free of difficult images, its strength lies in the manifest grief that infuses it, and in the skill which drives that emotion home. Here is the power of the Spanish tongue at its most compact:

It begins, fatefully,

At five in the afternoon.
It was sharp five in the afternoon.
A boy brought the white sheet
at five in the afternoon.
A basket of lime already prepared
at five in the afternoon.
The rest was death and only death
at five in the afternoon.

It ends with what might be the poet's own epitaph,

It will be a long time before there is born, if ever,
An Andalusian so clear, so rich in adventure,
I sing his elegance with words that moan
And I remember a breeze sad in the olive trees.

That year in Spain was bad. The Republic, which had come into power three years earlier with parades, flowers and singing, now found difficult opposition. Its prime minister, Manuel Azaña, who had played so prominent a part in bringing it to life, gave way to a wily old politician named Alejandro Lerroux who had been outwardly an advocate of a Republican government all his life. But not just any Republican government. He wanted one that he would run, one in which he could make the deals and reap the profits. In an autumn election the fickle voters defeated Azaña to support Lerroux; the Republic's "black biennium" began. The depression that had hit New York in 1929 came to Madrid in 1934, politically as well as financially. Men out of work begged on the streets of Madrid; they did it not politely as in the old days, with a humble bow and a "God bless you" for those who dropped a coin in a hat. Four of these beggars, both arrogant and impertinent, would carry a sheet by the four corners and make it quite clear that passers-by were expected to fill it with coins. One man at each corner solicited gifts from pedestrians in a tone that was more a command than a petition. *Madrileños* were not amused. Some were angry, some so ashamed that even a news photographer—a breed that ordinarily shows no qualms at any request—refused to take a photograph when he heard that it would go to a New York newspaper.

Meanwhile political tempers rose. The basic quarrel between conservatives and progressives which had preceded the Republic surged up again in terms far more bitter than those that had preceded the voting in 1931. Sharp differences of opinion were complicated by a split within Republican forces which, while cheering Monarchists, drove Republicans to extreme words and more extreme measures. All this was exacerbated by internal economic difficulties within the country, difficulties which tended to be blamed on Republicans instead of on the world economic slump. To these forces, making for trouble, were added European currents set in motion by Nazis in Germany and Fascists in Italy; these set up repercussions in Spain, and drove some of the moderate friends of the Republic to shelter under the cloak of Communism.

All this ferment had its effect even in the most apolitical quarters, from Andalusia in the south to the Basque and Galician regions in the north. In October 1934 the Basque miners went on strike, and while labor tactics in that country of stubborn geography and sullen weather are always grim, these proved ferocious as well as determined. In Catalonia sympathizers took to scattered shooting at symbols of what was later to be called "the establishment," including night trains.

The effect of all this political ferment on Federico is best revealed in his letters. His friend Morla Lynch, the diplomat, pictures the scene as it worsened in October: "Revolution in the Asturias; assassination of King Alexander in Marseilles which provoked also the death of Louis Barthou, French Minister of Foreign Affairs; death of M. Raymond Poincaré of France and of Ramón y Cajal" (a famous scientist in Spain).

"Federico came to see me," the Chilean continued. "We went to the last bullfight to be held in the old ring, and we did it not so much to see the bulls as to bid the old arena farewell. We were full of the sadness and nostalgia at the end of an era. . . ." On the 4th of November Federico read his tribute to Sánchez Mejías, the *Lament for the Death of a Bullfighter,* to the Morla family. "When he folded his manuscript, no one of us could speak. There are supreme moments in which emotion imposes a silence which says more than words. The only thing we could do was put the arm around the shoulder.

"And Federico stayed very late . . . talking about what comes after, that great question which rises gigantic on our horizon as we advance; the definitive reply never comes."

In late November Irene Lewisohn of New York City, who had long been the angel of the Neighborhood Playhouse on Grand Street, saw Federico's play *Blood Wedding* in Spain and fell in love with it. She decided she must have it for her Grand Street Playhouse.

In the midst of negotiations for the play, Miss Lewisohn gave a tea party for the playwright in her Madrid hotel. The setting was formal. So was Federico. Three years had passed since his New York experience. Home only six months from his great success in Buenos Aires, he was clearly marked by that success. Gone, for the moment, was the ebullient poet that so many New Yorkers remembered. Slender (for the first time), exceedingly well-tailored, completely self-possessed, saying little and smiling less, this was an entirely new Federico. Contact with cultivated and diplomatic life in Madrid and Buenos Aires had given him a formal polish. Society had fashioned his manners to her demands. Courteous, correct, chilly, he gave the impression of being an *enfant gaté* of the aristocracy, a bit bored by it all. If this was a role, it was, as usual, played superbly. It may, of course, have been a pose suggested by the wealth of Miss Lewisohn and the exciting prospect of having *Blood Wedding* played in New York. The role may have gone only skin deep. But there it was, and to an old friend it carried a shock. Gone the old infectious warmth and informal gaiety of Federico, replaced by the cool courtesy of the worldly and successful playwright popular on three continents. It all brought back Norma Brickell's comment when she saw him returned from Cuba, "I liked the old one better."

Later in November Miss Lewisohn returned to New York with José Weissberger's translation of *Blood Wedding* in hand. He was a friendly art expert who had lived long in Madrid, one of those polyglot internationalists who moved easily from one tongue to another. In this instance, that facility was his undoing. Miss Lewisohn asked an American friend to read the translation. Was it as good a play as she had thought? Certainly it was. But the translation? Beautiful and poetic. Critics might complain that it was too close to the Spanish to be thoroughly understandable by American audiences. Its beauty was the beauty of Spanish prose and poetry as well as of plot, and therefore it might not be easy for Americans to accept.

To one who knew both languages, the translation had great charm. But it was, after all, only half way through to idiomatic English. How would it sound to ears that knew no Spanish?

These doubts, haltingly expressed, did not discourage Miss Lewisohn. Weissberger's translation of the play was given a strange English title, *Bitter Oleander,* which said very little to those who went to see it. Played in the Lyceum Theater by Miss Lewisohn's Neighborhood Playhouse Company, the staging was handsome, the direction highly stylized. So was the acting. The whole passionate Spanish tragedy was played formally as masque, almost a ballet, with the translator's half Spanish, half English prose running through the action rather than dominating it. From time to time the audience, never really caught by the play's dramatic texture, laughed at an inept phrase. They found the mother's passionate way of addressing her beloved son as "my carnation" merely funny. *Bitter Oleander* in New York was not the *Bodas de Sangre* that had stirred Buenos Aires to torrents of enthusiasm. Nor was the audience prepared to accept it in English translation.

In Madrid Federico had finished *Yerma.* The company of Margarita Xirgu opened it on the 29th of December at the *Teatro Español.* It got critical praise, but in the hands of actors who were sometimes less than subtle its underlying beauties failed to move the audience. Even though played at home in the language in which Federico had written it, the production won no more than a pale acclaim. Played in New York in an experimental theater many years later, it lacked even that. So alien to modern ways of thinking and acting in the United States is the argument of the frustrated wife that the play at times took on a tinge of the absurd; this became so sharp that even *Yerma's* verbal beauty could not save it from a shrug and a laugh.

It was not until 1972, almost four decades after it had been written, that the play came to life with a surrealist setting and direction which created sensations both in Madrid and New York. In the latter city a simultaneous translation into English was provided by way of radio for those who knew no Spanish.

The year 1935 was a busy year and for Federico in the main a happy one, full of work and the fruit of work in the form of publication and production. Political skies continued to darken, but the theatrical world played Lorca dramas and replayed them. The sheer list of events is startling in its richness.

On January 1 Federico declared his new play, *Destruction of Sodom (Destrucción de Sodomo),* to be almost done. This was to be the third in a trilogy of barren love, a theme that had long obsessed him. If it was finished, it has not been seen publicly in print or on the stage. (The manuscript is rumored to sit hidden in a Madrid safe deposit box.) Later in the month, he directed for the *Club Anfistora* (which had staged *Don Perlimplín* earlier) a production of Lope de Vega's famous play of political struggle, *Peribañez y el Comendador de Ocaña;* he also harmonized folk songs to be included in it.

To fill out the customary theatrical three hours, he read his essay on *Tradition and Perspective of the Spanish Theater (Tradición y Perspective del Teatro Español).* No such title appears among the essays included in the poet's collected work, but a bit later he made one informal talk about the theater which contains this statement of his firm conviction: "The theater is one of the most expressive and useful instruments for the edification of a country; it is also the barometer which marks its greatness or its descent. A theater which is sensitive and well oriented in all its branches, from tragedy to vaudeville, can in a few years change the sensibility of the people; and a theater which has been destroyed, in which cloven hooves take the place of wings, can put to sleep an entire nation." This was Federico's dramatic creed.

The playwright went on to develop his thought in a way which might well be directed to New York today. "A people that does not aid and encourage its theater is moribund if not dead; the theater which does not gather to itself the best of society and of history, the drama of its people and the genuine color of its landscape and its spirit, with laughter or with tears, does not deserve to call itself theater, but is rather a place for that horrible thing which is called killing time."

This *charla,* this talk appears to have been given in February 1935 when the company of Margarita Xirgu, then playing *Yerma,* gave a special two o'clock in the morning performance for an audience of actors drawn from other theaters in Madrid. Obviously intended to instill in these theater people a sense of purpose over and above their nightly roles, it was also a statement of Federico's deep belief in the meaning and mission of the theater—a belief which he had stated in other ways and at other times, but never so forcibly.

Later in the month the actress Lola Membrives, who had played *Blood Wedding* in Buenos Aires, brought a revival of the play to Madrid. Then came one of Federico's puppet plays, *The Puppet Play of Don Cristóbal* in which the author himself operated the puppets as he had done long ago in Granada. These puppet plays deserve more attention than is ordinarily given them in acconts of Federico's work. They are the direct descendants of the *títeres,* the marionettes of his childhood, seen in village fairs and adopted by Federico for his own delight. The one he did in Granada in 1922 was the first of which we have record. The later *Don Cristóbal* of 1935 was a remake of *The Tragedy of Don Cristóbal and Señora Rosita (La Tragedia de Don Cristóbal y la Señora Rosita),* using the same characters and some of the same text. It was written in 1931, and so popular were the lusty theme and the violent puppet action that another version was prepared (after Federico's death) for the amusement of Republican soldiers in the Spanish Civil War. There is in it even a cousinship with *The Shoemaker's Prodigious Wife* which its author described as "a violent farce," and which Lola Membrives and her company played in Madrid a month later.

Doña Rosita the Spinster also came to blossom that month. Federico read it to his friends, and it was played in December, when Margarita Xirgu opened a season with it in Barcelona. This wistful, sentimental tragedy of the 19th century orphan maiden whose lover goes to South America promising to come back, but never keeps his promise, was an immediate success. It opened on December 12th in the *Teatro Principal* of Barcelona, and a special performance weeks later was given for the Florists Union. Members arriving at the theater were laden with enormous bouquets, which made them look as though they meant to be a floral setting for the play. At Christmas, Federico told the artists and writers of Catalonia, assembled at a banquet to do him honor, that he was going to Mexico for a theatrical season with Margarita Xirgu, who was to star in his plays there. It was a fine idea, and had he carried it out, it would have saved his life.

In many ways the months in Buenos Aires, with what was left of 1934 when he got back to Madrid, and the year 1935–36 in Spain represented the height of Federico's triumph. His six months in 1936 saw the completion of his surrealist play, *Thus Let Five Years Pass,* and his stern and firmly constructed tragedy, *The House of Bernarda Alba (La Casa de Bernarda Alba).* This latter is completely a prose play. No sooner had he finished it than he began dreaming of going back to poetry in its strict and classical form; he also told a poet friend that he was going to compose a book of sonnets to be called *Sonnets of Dark Love (Sonetos de Amor Oscuro).* That title smacked of Shakespeare, but the sonnets that made their appearance under it contained no Dark Lady. They are, however, authentically dark, very pained, sunless and dimly beautiful. That he had been able to complete all this work in the first half of 1936 is a tribute to the strength of his creative powers and to that ability for hard work which he had learned to develop in his adult years.

The atmosphere of Spain at the time was heavily, portentously political, with the Republic shadowed by reactionary clouds and its statesmen unable to see their most important problems or to solve them. In April the poet lost control of his beloved jitney theater *La Barraca.* A reactionary student group won the conservative government's permission to take it over; it played in Barcelona without its creator's sanction or participation. Federico resigned. This was a few days after he had given an interview to the Madrid paper, *La Voz,* in which he outlined his plan to present Spain's social problems in the theater, playing them in a socialist setting. The political pestilence which afflicted Europe, and by extension the Iberian peninsula, was beginning to infect this least political of poets and dramatists. Intensely aware of human suffering, resentful of pressures and powers, he struck out where and as he could, and sometimes made trouble for himself when he only had meant to protest against pain inflicted on others. He was, even as he approached his forties, a political innocent, of whose genius his fatherland might be expected to have been conscious and careful.

But political storms of the kind that were blowing up in Spain in the 1930s did not discriminate between poetic geniuses and common politicians. Federico's friendships, his sponsors, his sympathies, his companions were with the Republic. His theatrical invention, *La Barraca,* was subsidized by the Republic. His speech was not always neutral, nor confined to literary matters, and everything he said or did was subject to analysis by enemies of that Republic. Moreover, in his home town of Granada he had made, during the course of his witty and articulate life, both devoted friends and bitter enemies. Had he been able to escape political persecution, it would have been a miracle.

A score of prominent political figures were jailed, including Lorca's old friend, Don Fernando de los Rios. So turbulent were political affairs that in the last three months of 1935 Spain had three Cabinets. The general lines of the revolt which would break out in July 1936 are said to have been laid down during the relative quiet of 1935, but the moment for that revolt came slowly. It would take months of disorder, strikes, church burning, political chaos, and the final shooting of the conservative Calvo Sotelo before the people were stirred to the point of open organized offense and defense.

And Federico? The state of mind of private citizens, having to live day by day on rumor of armed revolt, can be imagined. In January the poet took the fatal negative step of deciding that he would not make the announced trip to Mexico. Why he changed his mind and stayed in Spain is another of those small, but vital, mysteries that dot his life. Early that year he told a reporter, "I am waiting for a cable from Margarita Xirgu. It will come this month. I plan to go directly to New York, where I lived a year. I want to see some old friends of mine, Yankees, who are friends of Spain. . . . From New York I am going straight to Mexico. Five days by train. What a delight! Things change, landscapes and sad cows. But no one talks to me. . . . In Mexico I will attend my openings, and give a lecture on Quevedo. What an injustice Quevedo has suffered! He is Spain's most interesting poet! . . . I will talk about Quevedo in Mexico, for Quevedo is Spain." But he neither went, nor talked about Quevedo.

12

CHAPTER

The Crime Was in Granada

FEDERICO'S LONG HABIT WAS TO join his family in Andalusia during mid-July and to spend the summer there. His father and mother, his sister Concha (married to Manuel Montesinos, an old friend and former member of *El Rinconcillo* who had risen under the Republic to be Mayor of Granada) were expecting him in the pleasant family house called *La Huerta de San Vicente,* outside of Granada.

Friends in Madrid warned him that in the growing state of national hysteria Granada might be a dangerous place. But who can imagine that one's dearly loved summer house holds perils? Wouldn't it be safer to go home, where everyone knew him, than to stay in the riotous capital?

On the afternoon of the 15th Federico sought reassurance in reaching back to his youth with a visit to an old schoolteacher, Don Antonio Rodriquez Espinosa, who had been his friend since 1902 when the four-year-old was brought by his mother to his first school. Loving a joke, he announced himself to the maid servant by the absurd name of Homovono Picadillo, and then, when his puzzled host appeared, joined in mutual laughter. "I came to say farewell, Don Antonio," he announced. "Tomorrow I go to Granada." The teacher, who had watched the funeral of Calvo Sotelo the day before, shook his head. He had seen 2,000 people shouting vengeance as the coffin passed, and the sight still terrified his memory. It was a bad moment to go, a bad moment to stay.

That night Federico, still undecided, read his new play, *The House of Bernarda Alba,* to friends of a well-known physician, Dr. Eusebio Oliver. For the moment, normalcy seemed to return.

The next day, in response to a telephone call, his friend Rafael Martínez Nadal went to fetch him from the Lorca family apartment at 102 Calle Alcalá and take him to lunch at the Martínez house. Three times they were stopped between the Lorca front door and the neighboring taxi stand by people who wanted to shake Federico by the hand. "Going out with you is worse than walking with a famous bullfighter!" laughed Rafael.

At lunch with his friend's family the question of going to Granada or staying in Madrid kept coming up. He told them that his family had already left for Granada, and he hated to stay in the apartment alone. They offered him the refuge of a bedroom ordinarily occupied by a Martínez Nadal brother who was at the moment in Barcelona. Federico thanked them, but shook his head. "I would love to stay with you, but the 18th of July is my name day, and that of my father. Neither my brother Paco nor my little sister Isabel is at home this year. If I don't go, my parents will be terribly disappointed."

The two men argued the point over after-lunch cognac. Rafael had just returned from a lecture trip to Scandinavia, where he had told enthusiastic audiences about Federico's poems and plays. Lorca tried to persuade his friend to accompany him to Granada, but in vain. Finally, observing grimly that "These fields are going to fill with the dead," Federico put out his freshly lighted cigarette and stood up. "I've made up my mind. I'm going to Granada, and in God's hands be it."

On this somber note, the two friends went to Cook's to buy a railroad ticket. Federico talked gaily of his plans to finish *The Destruction of Sodom,* and then another on the biblical theme of Thamar and her brother Amnon, which he had already touched in a poem. They stopped in a bookstore to buy Lorca volumes which Rafael was to send off to new-made friends in Scandinavia. They went to Alcalá, 102, in order to pack the poet's suitcase. That done (by Rafael), Federico went to his desk, took out a package, and handing it to his friend, said soberly, "Keep this for me. If anything happens to me, destroy it all. If not, give it to me when next we meet." It was the gesture, and almost the words, with which Lorca had entrusted a similar package to Philip Cummings in Vermont six years earlier. The difference was that Martínez Nadal, unlike Cummings, opened his package the moment he got home. In it were personal papers, and what seemed to be a first draft of five scenes of the much discussed *The Public.* Writing about the incident more than thirty years later, Martínez Nadal states his conviction that Federico's charge to destroy the package in case anything untoward happened could not have been meant to apply to the manuscript. In any event, he kept it.

Then they went to the train. Going to the train in Spain, in those days, was a ceremony accompanied with much embracing, much back-slapping, much conversation. This time things were different. In Federico's sleeping compartment he autographed his books for the Scandinavians; Martínez Nadal promised to see that they went off. A man passed down the corridor, and laughter ceased. Federico shook both fists. "That's a deputy from Granada, a man of bad omen, a bad person. Look, Rafael, go now, and don't wait until the train leaves. I'm going to close the curtains and go to bed so that animal neither sees me nor talks to me."

The next morning he reached his home station. All was quiet. He went at once to *La Huerta de San Vicente* where he found his parents and his sister Concha, his grand piano, his familiar whitewashed room, his huge oaken writing table. But in Granada all was not as peaceful as this suburb looked. That night the radio announced that Gil Robles, head of a powerful Republican group called CEDA, had crossed the northern Spanish border to join his wife and son at Biarritz. This did not surprise the listeners—Gil Robles had never been a strong man—but it sounded ominous. The next announcement was worse. "A few moments ago the veteran Commander of the Spanish Foreign Legion, General Francisco Franco, launched over the Canary Islands radio a call to uprising. This was directed to the army of Morocco." The García Lorcas looked at each other in horror. The threat was now the fact. The Republic, their Republic, would soon be under armed attack.

What happened between that 17th of July when Federico arrived home and the 19th of August is a tangled web of safety and terror, friendship and treachery that, in happier days, Federico himself might have made into a play. For a long time the details were obscured by the difficulties of communication in a nation being pushed into a civil war. The poet's friends in Madrid knew that he had gone home to Granada, and assumed that he was safe. On July 19th Seville fell into the hands of General Queipo de Llano, who hated intellectuals and said so publicly. General Franco was enlisting troops in Tetuan. Troops from Morocco landed at Cadiz and Algeciras. Franco declared a state of war, and demanded that the legitimate Republican government in Madrid surrender under threat of being bombed. The government refused to be terrorized. The people, under the democratic illusion that the government was theirs, demanded arms.

The fever of rebellion spread quickly from Seville to Granada. Franco's political supporters, the Falange, began to fill the streets. For the moment, the Republican governor of Granada province, Torres Martínez, held fast, refusing to yield under pressure. The town's mayor, Manuel Montesinos (Federico's brother-in-law), found himself suddenly faced by his people with a demand for arms to fight off the rebels. Staunchly devoted to the Republic, he refused to favor individual adventurers and asked for the formation of small groups, responsibly led, to occupy strategic points of the city and keep a careful eye on dubious elements.

This would have been a course both intelligent and responsible had the situation been less dangerous. But matters moved too fast. On July 20th the rebel troops, commanded by two colonels and a captain, entered the city at the sacred hour of siesta when the populace was generally asleep. They killed the only policeman who was visible, and proceeded to "clean up" the defenseless town. They arrested Montesinos and put him in the provisional jail along with other "enemies of the true Spain." It was too late for intelligent defense. In less than half an hour troops had occupied the lower part of the city and the hill of the Alhambra. Only the opposite hill, the Albaicín, occupied by gypsies and workers, held out.

Then came a larger and more confused terror, as the process of "cleaning up" spread from the Falange to such competing groups as the Requetes, the members of Young Spain (made up of reactionary students), the Black Squadron and any other lovers of violence who could get guns from the rebels. Violence, becoming competitive, became irresponsible. No one, however famous or popular, was safe, not even a beloved children's doctor. Men were taken out of their homes, killed on impulse, out of a desire for revenge or a love of sadism. Grudges had free rein. It was easy enough for any man to be "suspected" of opposing the new rebels and their bitter passion to "reform" the Republic. All of Spain's deep anger against the hard conditions of its life, all its inherited resentments, its addiction to sparring with death, came to the front. Everyone's life was imperiled. It was safe neither to go into the streets nor to cower at home. With Mayor Montesinos in jail, his wife and children took refuge in the *Huerta de San Vicente,* but the new "police" kept insisting that the Mayor was also with the Lorca family, and harassing the Lorca house. Not even Don Federico García's solid and substantial reputation saved his home from search or the members of his family from suspicion. None of them were active political people except Concha's husband, but they were known not only to have a mayor in the family but to be warm friends of that important official of the Republic, Don Fernando de los Rios, Minister of Education and then Ambassador of the Spanish state to the United States. The poet son of the family, young Federico, wore strange clothes, made fun of the city's elders (he had never been forgiven the ridicule expressed in *Gallo* and was suspected of even more outrageous ideas).

One morning in August the midday mail at San Vicente brought an anonymous letter addressed to Federico which shocked the family and doubly shocked the much loved elder son. It berated the poet for being immoral, irreligious and a demagogue. Whatever substance might have been found for the first two charges, the third was clearly absurd, but words at a time like that lose solid meaning and become weapons. The letter ended with a threat to kill.

A few hours later two men bearing revolvers came to the house and demanded—not Federico, but the gardener's son, who was charged with helping to burn a church at Asqueroso. Luckily he had departed, but when Federico tried to tell them so, they cursed him, punched him in the face, and told him they knew all about *him.*

The implications of the letter and the blows were too terrifying to be disregarded. Clearly Federico was no longer safe in his father's home. Where would he be safe? He could not go away—Franco's sympathizers controlled the roads, and to try to flee across the open *vega* would be suicide. With all their lifelong friends, was there nobody in the new regime to whom they could turn for counsel, if not for refuge?

They thought of one, a young poet named Luís Rosales, a friend and admirer of Federico. He was politically conservative, and he had three brothers, Miguel, José and Antonio, who were active devotees of the uprising, so active that they were known to have filled their rooms with weapons and turned them into veritable arsenals. Could Luís' friendship be relied on? Could he persuade his impassioned brothers to honor the sacred demands of hospitality and stand solidly behind the needs of his greatly loved friend?

A telephone call summoned Luís to San Vicente on the 5th or the 9th of August. The Lorca family in council laid before him the peril and the problem. Where could Federico go to be safe? The first suggestion was the house of Maestro de Falla. But Don Manuel was an ardent Catholic, and he had quarreled with Federico over the latter's "Ode to the Most Holy Sacrament." Moreover all Granada knew that Federico and the musician had been warm friends. Any search for the poet would surely reach the latter's house. Nor would Federico consent to have his old friend endangered. "Falla? No."

Could Luís take Federico past the Franco lines to safety on the other side? Too dangerous at the moment.

"Meanwhile, he can come to my house," said Luís suddenly, swallowing whatever doubts he must have had. "I will engage to persuade my brothers." At a moment when ideas were scarce, this generous offer sounded like a possible refuge. Surely no one would suspect a house of harboring a suspect where the sons were so actively engaged in forwarding the Movement.

It seemed a dubious, and dangerous, solution, but time pressed and better ideas were lacking. Tearful family farewells followed quickly, and Federico, crouched down in the back seat of Luís' car, went off to the Rosales house. Nobody interfered. Streets leading to the Calle del Angulo were deserted. Arriving at the house, Luís went in first. All was quiet. Federico followed, and the door closed solidly behind them.

At the moment, none of the other brothers was at home. Federico was installed on the second floor, in the apartment of an aged aunt, Doña Luisa Camacho. Peace returned to the spirit of the threatened poet, except at night, when he and Luís listened to the radio news of deepening horrors. The rebellion was digging in, consolidating its scattered victories. Workers in the Albaicín had surrendered. The city councillors and their aides had been shot, all but two. Luís concealed from Federico the fact that Concha's husband, the Mayor, was one of the victims. He was shot on August 10th.

The three older brothers had been persuaded only grudgingly that the demands of friendship and hospitality were greater than those of politics. For more than a week a relative peace subsisted in the Rosales house, and particularly in the second floor apartment of Doña Luisa. The room was quiet, the Rosales library was ample. Federico spent most of his days reading and writing. Security seemed to have returned and to be dependable.

Then, on August 16th at five in the afternoon (that

fatal hour for the poet's friend Ignacio Sánchez Mejías) the doorbell rang. One Ramón Ruiz Alonso, a brutal and fantastic typographer who now held a minor post in the Black Squadron, asked loudly for Federico García Lorca. The whole house listened. Ruiz Alonso was no friend of the family; he was known to be a curiously warped character whose frustrations took themselves out in sudden and relentless violence. The office of his paper, *El Ideal,* had been burned by men of the Republic when the rebels first entered Granada. For reasons that are still obscure he is said to have made his pursuit of Federico a personal vendetta. He had repeatedly visited San Vicente, demanding the poet; refused information, he had even maltreated its aged master. Finally he had stumbled on an inadvertent phrase that led him to the Rosales house. He demanded to see the poet.

The Rosales brothers were not at home. In the lower hall Doña Luisa staunchly denied that such a person was in the house. There was surely some mistake. She must call the oldest (and most fanatic) brother, Miguel. Meanwhile, what was Ruiz Alonso doing here, making demands in a house known to be helping the rebels? The under-officer of the Black Squadron pushed aside her protests and her person. Unhampered by any barrier of courtesy, he searched the house, room by room. On an upper balcony reading, in pajamas, he found the poet.

Meanwhile, Miguel arrived in answer to his aunt's phone call. Here the record grows dimmer. What must have been the confused irritation of this devoted rebel, called by his aunt and his brother Luís to protect a poet for whom he had little regard? He had consented, however unwillingly, to his family's gesture of sanctuary to his brother's friend, a known member of the Republic's "establishment." By this act, was not he himself implicated and endangered? Now he was confronted with the brutal insistence of a fellow rebel that the poet must face charges. Were he to refuse cooperation, he and all his family would be brought under suspicion of lukewarm devotion to the rebel cause. Moreover, the rebellious splinter groups were themselves at war, and even he could not be sure of reaching authorities who would sympathize with his devotion to older family loyalties.

The assumption of those who ask fairness in judging the Rosales brothers is that they themselves, in the confused and competitive state of the new rebellion, had absolutely no choice. Either they must give Federico up to the authorities then in control of the most power, or their own lives would be in acute danger. Under the implacable demands of the printer Ruiz Alonso, Miguel capitulated. Federico was taken out of the house and off to government headquarters, where he joined the terrified crowd of victims awaiting "justice" from Commander Valdés, whose favorite and most frequent decision was "Shoot him." As a priest told an English inquirer, "Valdés would have shot Jesus and His Mother Mary if they had appeared before him." Federico García Lorca, poet and dramatist famous on three continents, who had celebrated in wonderful words the recognition of death as a constant factor in life, now saw death, petty, irrelevant, inescapable, waiting for him by way of a dirty corridor.

The facts of those who have tried to disentangle the faded record and find out what happened to Federico, hour by hour, do not entirely agree. The activity of the Rosales brothers is obscure. Their sturdy aunt, Doña Luisa, is said to have sent food, tobacco and a blanket to Federico by a young baker, who hardly recognized him, so greatly had terror changed his features. Presumably it was Doña Luisa who telephoned the Lorca family and Manuel de Falla to tell them what was happening. The Lorca family was too important and, under ordinary circumstances, too influential in Granada to suffer unprotesting the arrest of a son. But at this tangled moment, when power itself was impassioned and in conflict, importance and influence in the failing hands of known Republicans counted for nothing. Even the world-famous musician Maestro Falla could not make himself heard.

Questions still surround the final act. There seems to be no doubt that the most famous Spanish poet of the 20th century was detained from the 16th to the 18th of August, and then, with or without trial, was taken out of government headquarters and shot at dawn on the 19th of August with a group of known victims who were charged as he was, and perhaps with no more reason, with being enemies of the new rebel regime. Where he was shot, where he lies buried, no one surely knows. The most credible assumption is that he lies in a common burial ground at Viznar, a miserable village outside of Granada, where the bully boys of the Falange had a meeting house. His grave is marked no more clearly than that of his companions in the common pit.

Was the killing of so well-known a figure as horridly casual as it sounds? Or was there someone, some group, some higher power directed consciously at Federico and basically responsible for his death? Did a radio conversation between Valdés and the Machiavellian General Queipo de Llano in Seville actually take place, and was it the General who doomed Lorca? Was this one of those chance tragedies that happened when violent forces compete and collide? Was the printer Ruiz Alonso with his frustrated hatreds really the ultimate villain who brought Federico down? Or was he the low-grade tool of some hidden foe more worthy of his victim? One can guess endlessly, and people have, but no one seems surely to know. The meaningless death cries out for an important villain, and indeed the elaborate excuses in which the

Falange indulged after the attention of a horrified world had been focussed on the killing might make one suspect that such an ugly one did in fact exist. But who was he? The question still sounds.

And there are lesser questions. Whether the Rosales brothers were as deeply protective and distressed as many think them, whether the older ones, schizophrenic under the double pressure of family loyalty and political fervor, have now hidden their actions behind the devotion of the younger one who was openly Federico's friend and admirer, who now knows? Luís was booed in Latin America when he tried to tell how hard he worked to save the poet's life. And what does it all matter, so late in the story?

Federico once wrote a poem containing these lines—

Mother, when I die
Let these men know it
Send blue telegrams
To go from South to North.

But his mother was too shattered to send telegrams anywhere, and even if she had tried to reach his friends in North and South, the Franco terrorists would not have permitted it. News was travelling slowly under censorship in war-torn Spain. Not until September 12th, three weeks after the assassination, did word of the catastrophe get as far as embattled Madrid, and then neither the press nor the public could believe that it was true. Rumors were invented on every street corner. Errors were more frequent than facts. *El Sol,* the city's leading newspaper, thought at first that the poet's famous name had been confused with that of his brother-in-law, the Mayor of Granada. Two days later the execution of Federico was confirmed: death had come not only to Montesinos but to "our glorious poet."

The outside world was equally lacking in information, equally aghast at the rumors. Writers everywhere rallied to find out the truth. As late as October 14th a telegram went from London to the military authorities of Granada: "H. G. Wells, President of the PEN Club of London, anxiously awaits news of his distinguished colleague, the poet Federico García Lorca, and would be deeply grateful if you would send them." An answer came back, unhurried, from a Colonel Espinosa. "I do not know where Don Federico García Lorca can be found." Newspaper men queried General Franco, who shrugged the crime away as "a bit of gossip."

On a day in early autumn a reporter friend stopped me in the corridor of the Commodore Hotel in New York. He had just come back from Spain, and after a word or two he said, "I'm so sorry about your friend." "What friend?" I asked, startled. "The poet Federico García Lorca." And I, still ignorant, asked, "What happened to him? I've been out of town and away from newspapers." "The Fascists shot him. Didn't you know?" The corridor whirled.

Then came Bob Neville's story. He had been staying in Granada in the Hotel Washington Irving (that beehive ceiling, and the poet's strong, square hands on the keys of the old piano!); very early in the morning, while it was still dark, he had heard the feet of men marching up the hill. Later that day he had been told that Federico García Lorca had been shot. There was a cemetery at the top of the hill, and he thought that he had heard Federico march up past his window in the old hotel to die at the top of his beloved Alhambra hill. Later investigations do not agree with that, but Bob Neville still bore the shock of the marching sound at early dawn, and the later report which persuaded him that the famous and beloved poet had been among the marchers.

Had the news appeared in the New York papers? "No, but an English reporter named Waithman got a dispatch printed in the *London News Chronicle.*" At once I wrote Mr. Waithman and got back a copy of his dispatch. It told the bare fact of the execution but gave no details. I wrote the State Department. They had no word from their Madrid representative of the death of this famous poet. Had it been France, matters might have been different, but few American Ambassadors are known for their interest in the literature of the land to which they are assigned. Anyhow, Federico was gone, and why bother them for details? The war was still producing plenty of other executions.

Another, older poet, Antonio Machado, told what no official, no reporter said:

The crime was in Granada.
They killed Federico as the first light came
The squad of executioners
Dared not look him in the face.
All of them closed their eyes.
They prayed, but not even God saves you!
Federico fell dead,
Blood in the face and lead in the bowels
Know, then, that the crime was in Granada
Poor Granada—in his Granada.

AFTERWORD

TO MOST LOVERS OF SPANISH poetry, Machado had the final word about Federico. Other friends—French and English—anguished by this death, have for various reasons sought more details. Marie Laffranque, Marcelle Auclair, Jean-Louis Schonberg, Claude Couffon in France, and the British Gerald Brennan and Ian Gibson (the latter lived for a year in Granada to track down patiently every event, every person, every hint) have come to their own separate conclusions or their own speculations. Gibson, whose recent book is *La Represión Nacionalista de Granada en 1936, y la Muerte de Federico García Lorca,* believes that the actual assassination took place outside the city of Granada, not far from Viznar, near the famous Fuente Grande, the Arab Aindamar (Spring of Tears). There, with three other men who were also shot without mercy at the same time, the poet-dramatist was buried in a narrow trench, under one of his favorite objects, an ancient olive tree.

To possess this final bit of fact may comfort those who must know or remain forever with a question gnawing at their minds. Others feel, as does Federico's friend of Eden days, that the search for post-mortem detail becomes merely "an ugly statistic," whereas "My memories and my dedication and my joy is with a living wonderful spirit, unquenched and unquenchable."

To those who were not fortunate enough to have known Federico in person, there are certain aspects of his work that still call for comment. And this in spite of the volumes written in many countries about the work and its author.

The first of these aspects is the importance of Lorca's two American trips, one north and one south, on his work, a subject which has been largely neglected by European and even American critical appraisals. The second is the effect of the surrealist philosophy on Federico's later plays, and particularly on his unpublished but much discussed *The Public.*

There can be no doubt that in Lorca's adult progress, and particularly in the development of his plays, the American experience had notable psychological effects. Some of these are directly visible; others take the form of contradiction or retreat. The major theme that runs through most of them is, of course, frustration, particularly for women, but also for men. If he felt masculine frustration throughout his own life, he was also an extremely acute observer of frustration in women. Much of this latter may have begun more or less unconsciously while he was in his mother's care as a small child, but with or without her he never lost it. In Fuente Vaqueros, in Granada, women could not run their lives as they wished because men interfered. There and elsewhere, men could not run their lives as they wished because women interfered.

This motif began to show itself most clearly during and after Lorca's American trips. If it was frustration, as some friends say, that took him to the United States, frustration was surely his constant companion while he was there. To deprive him of the ability to talk and be understood, as did the English-speaking habits of this country, was to stifle him and force him to find release in some form of protest. This quickly made itself felt not only in his New York poems but also in the plays that followed. In *Don Perlimplín,* in *The Shoemaker's Prodigious Wife,* in *Yerma* and *Blood Wedding,* most pointedly in the stark tragedy of *Bernarda Alba,* frustration is the cause and keynote of the drama. In the surrealist subtleties of *Thus*

Let Five Years Pass and *The Public* this theme may be developed in a more complicated manner, but it is still unmistakable.

His own personal frustrations have been noted in earlier pages. He could not escape his earlier reputation of imitating an older poet. He could not escape his father's insistence that he study law, the family's insistence that he find a recognized creditable occupation, the pressure of the morality and conventions of Granada, the galling dependence on his family which lasted until after he was thirty. Some of these he outgrew as he progressed, but deeper frustrations of sex and of achievement pursued him all his life.

If for Federico himself frustration was by long personal experience the major theme and practice of life, it had to be countered in some measure and by some endurable device if life was to continue. His own recourse was to write, and in writing either to express his frustration or to retreat into the life that had surrounded him in his childhood.

This swing back and forth between frustration and his favorite forms of retreat and compensation seems to have come most brilliantly to expression not in the starkly realistic *House of Bernarda Alba* in which frustration is the theme and keynote of the play, but in those that lean most surely on the surrealist aesthetic which freed him from conventional and accepted ways of thinking and speaking. Four of these are known to have existed. *Thus Let Five Years Pass* has been published and is available in English translation. It has been played, but with no great success. *The Dreams of My Cousin Aurelia (Los Sueños de Mi Prima Aurelia)* has apparently disappeared. *The Destruction of Sodom* (Dia I) is said to have been completed in January 1935; there is a rumor that a copy lies in a Madrid safe deposit box.

These latter two remain to a certain extent mysteries,

but gossip has them concerned chiefly with homosexual love. The third *avant-garde* play, and the one most discussed, is *The Public,* started in the spring of 1930 just after the author left New York (part of the manuscript he wrote on paper bearing the name of the Hotel Union in Havana).

This play has had a complicated history. Soon after he returned to Madrid from South America, Federico read an early version to three friends, Carlos Morla Lynch and his wife Bebe, and Rafael Martínez Nadal. The French writer, Marcelle Auclair, a friend of all of them, tells the effect of this surrealist drama on that sophisticated group. "Rafael had a very disagreeable memory of that evening," she says. "Carlos and Bebe, disconcerted by the first speeches, more and more bothered by the violence, the declared homosexuality of those first acts, let Federico read his play from start to finish without saying a word. At the end, Bebe was almost weeping, not from emotion, but from dismay.

" 'Federico, you are not going to have that played! It is impossible! Apart from the scandal, it is unplayable.'

"Lorca did not try to defend his piece. Down in the street he told Rafael, 'This is for the theater years from now. Until then, let's say no more about it.' "

But a great deal more has been said and will continue to be said. In 1933 Federico told an inquiring reporter in Buenos Aires that he did not expect to present *The Public* in Buenos Aires "nor any other place, for I believe there is no company which would be moved to take it to the stage and no public which would tolerate it without growing indignant." Asked why, he answered, "Because it is the mirror of the public. That is to say, it makes appear on stage what each of the characters is thinking, many times without being aware of it, while he looks at the play. And as the drama of everyone is at times biting and generally not honorable, the audience would rise and keep the play from going on. Yes, my piece is not to be played; it is, as I have already described it, a poem to be whistled at."

It has remained mostly a "poem to be whistled at" for nearly forty years. Fragments of it appear in the *Complete Works,* but not enough to be in any way satisfactory. In 1958 a draft copy "of labyrinthine confusion" came to Martínez Nadal, who still kept a far from happy memory of having heard Federico read it in 1930. After a great deal of study, of attempts to recall the atmosphere of 1930 when the play was written, of futile efforts to persuade the Lorca family (which is supposed to have another copy) that the time had come to bring the play to life, Martínez Nadal, in 1970, published an account of his study, his analysis of the play, with a set of accompanying and illustrative quotations. He published a version of the play in 1976.

This is a play within a play, says Martínez Nadal, "perhaps the first important attempt to apply surrealist techniques to a theater of human problems, alive both in the reality of life and in dreams."

In it, Lorca tried "a new form of dramatic expression, a drama of abstract ideas and passions, not of characters and argument in the traditional sense of those terms." "He starts," says Martínez Nadal, "from a concrete problem, homosexual love, to arrive at conclusions about love on all levels; he tears the masks from his characters in order to reach general conclusions about the mask or masks which each component of humanity wears; about the multiple personalities in hidden struggle which compose the supposed single personality of a man."

It is "a capital work, not only among Federico's plays but in terms of all that was written in Europe and America in the 1930s. It gives the poet a surprising, an immense dimension. The whole is so well constructed, so intimately linked, so perfectly balanced . . . that it is impossible to talk of it in fragments without danger of betraying it."

The first recorded attempt to stage *The Public* in the United States was made at the University of Texas in the early spring of 1972 when Martínez Nadal, lecturing there, described it in some detail. Students were wildly enthusiastic, declared *The Public* to be "Our play!"—insisted on producing the fragments that were given, and created scenes of real excitement over it. A project for translation by an English poet is now under discussion.

Until this mysterious play can be seen and appraised on the stage by a wider public, the full extent of the effect of surrealism on Lorca's drama must rest on the 1972 version of his old and mainly unappreciated *Yerma.* This he wrote in 1934, starting it in between his two American trips, and finishing it in Montevideo for a first night in Buenos Aires.

Yerma is a poetic tragedy of frustration; the heroine, Yerma, is a farmer's wife obsessed with the desire for a child; her husband is more interested in the yield of his flock and fields. The struggle of conflicting interests rises to such a point that she strangles him, thus defeating forever her chances of bearing the longed-for child. Played realistically in Montevideo and Madrid with only reasonable success, *Yerma* became notable in 1972, thirty-six years after its author's death, when it was presented in Madrid and then in New York as an *avant-garde* play in such a fashion as to win it international acclaim. Victor García, the producer, abolished all literal details of scene and stage furniture, and put in their place a dirt-colored trampolin on which characters moved as though walking on thick sand. The setting was of no color; its lifelessness became the symbolic background against which the tragic drama took on added strength and meaning. By mechanical means, in the Romería scene, this device was raised to become a mural background for the hanging vision of Yerma's inflamed dream. The performance brilliantly justified Federico's confidence in the powers of imagination when making use of surrealist means. In literal productions, *Yerma* had been poetic but not convincing. Here, with an *avant-garde* setting and interpretation, decades after its author had felt the first force of that theory, *Yerma* came into its own.

To suggest that these various specimens of Lorca's dramatic work owe their inspiration and the strength of their motive power to Lorca's two American trips, one north and the other south, is not to imply that he was at any time or in any way diverted from his lifelong preoccupation with Andalusia and with Spain. On the contrary, in getting far away from his native province and his native land, their contrasts with the new American hemisphere brought to him more clearly their obsessions and their problems.

At the same time, by exposing him to a different, much broader (and uglier) world, New York played a vital part in helping the poet to his late coming of age. His "Ode to Walt Whitman," his New York poems and his later plays showed him to have arrived at a degree of stature and compassion not hitherto apparent. He was now beginning to understand a world far wider than the agricultural one he had been born into, and to plumb it to the depths.

Only in the volume *Poet in New York* are there direct evidences of Federico's reaction to American scenes, and those are perhaps not exactly what an American might have wished. At the time of their printing, the United States was, perhaps, not sufficiently mature to look its slums, its Negro problem, its mass culture in the face.

Now that four decades and three wars have made their mark on this country, the Lorca poems about the United States take their proper place as social criticism in the moving form of great poetry. This he did for us. This the United States in its size, its crudities, its cruelties, its whole industrial structure did for him. The effect of South America is less visible. He wrote no book about Buenos Aires, but he wrote *Yerma* in that city.

The most important thing that the whole American experience did was to help Federico grow out of his sheltered childhood, his dependence on his family, his Granada, his Spain. If it brought him new frustrations, it helped him to conquer old ones, until Martínez Nadal could say, speaking of his last play, that "from Lorca's angle the laws—moral, human or divine—matter little. In the face of man's suffering, blood and death, moral precepts vanish into nothing."

Jorge Guillén was with him when he got back from both American experiences and heard him read his new play, *The House of Bernarda Alba.* "Now," said Federico, "I see what my theater is going to be," and Guillén observes, "He regarded his maturity as a kind of opening, as an entrance into his kingdom. . . . An ample future ahead of him. Toward it he marched with decision and joy. . . . What obstacles could stay him?"

In August of that summer the question was answered by the official assassin's bullet.

SELECTED BIBLIOGRAPHY

This book is based on conversations, comments and interviews with its subject, his family, his friends and his critics. To these sources must be added the printed testimony of books written about him and his work, most of them in Spanish. (Books mentioned in the text are marked with an asterisk*)

Albertí, Rafael. *La Arboleda Perdida.* Buenos Aires: Compañia General Fabril Editora SA, 1959.

*Auclair, Marcelle. *Enfances et Mort de García Lorca.* Paris: Edition du Seuil, 1968.

Barea, Arturo. *Lorca, the Poet and his People.* Translated by Ilse Barea. Cambridge: Bowes and Bowes, 1952.

Borkenau, Franz. *The Spanish Cockpit* (forword by Gerald Brenan). London: Faber and Faber Ltd., 1937.

Brenan, Gerald. *The Face of Spain.* London: Pelligrini and Cudahy, 1957.

Brickell, Herschel. "A Spanish Poet in New York." *Virginia Quarterly,* 21, 1945.

Campbell, Roy. *Lorca, an Appreciation of his Poetry.* Cambridge: Bowes and Bowes, 1952.

*Cano, José Luis. *Biografía Illustrada.* Barcelona: Ediciones Destino SL, 1962.

Crowe, John A. *Federico García Lorca.* Los Angeles: 1945.

Dalí, Ana Maria. *Salvador Dalí: Visto por su Hermana.* Barcelona: Editorial Juventud SA, 1949.

*Dalí, Salvador. *Secret Life of Salvador Dalí.* Translated by Haakon M. Chevalier. New York: Dial Press, 1942.

*De la Guardia, Alfredo. *García Lorca, Persona y Creación.* Buenos Aires: Editorial Schapire, 1944.

*Del Río, Angel. *Vida y Obra de Federico García Lorca.* Zaragoza: "Heraldo de Aragon," 1952.

**Gallo, Revista de Granada.* Granada: Number 1, February 1928; Number 2, April 1928.

Ganivet, Angel. *Granada la bella.* Helsinki: 1896.

*García Lorca, Federico. *From Lorca's Theater: Five Plays.* Translated by James Graham-Lujan and Richard O'Connell. New York: Charles Scribner's Sons, 1941.

*García Lorca, Federico. *Gypsy Ballads.* Translated by Rolfe Humphries. Bloomington: University of Indiana Press, 1953.

*García Lorca, Federico. *Lament for the Death of a Bullfighter.* Translated by A. A. Lloyd. New York: Oxford University Press, 1937.

*García Lorca, Federico. *Obras Completas.* Madrid: (4th edition) Aguilar SA de Ediciones, 1960.

*García Lorca, Federico. *Poems.* Translated by Stephen Spender and J. L. Gili. London: The Dolphin, 1939.

*García Lorca, Federico. *The Poet in New York, and other Poems of Federico García Lorca.* Translated by Rolfe Humphries. New York: W. W. Norton and Co., 1940.

*García Lorca, Federico. *Poet in New York.* Complete

Spanish text with a new translation by Ben Belitt. New York: Grove Press, 1935.

*García Lorca, Federico. *Songs.* Translated by Philip Cummings. Pittsburgh: Duquesne University Press, 1976.

*García Lorca, Federico. *Three Tragedies of Federico García Lorca.* Translated by James Graham-Lujan and Richard O'Connell. New York: New Directions, 1947.

*García Lorca, Francisco. *Angel Ganivet: su idea del hombre.* Buenos Aires: Editorial Losada SA, 1952.

Gibson, Ian. *The Death of Lorca.* Chicago: J. Philip O'-Hara, Inc., 1973.

*Gibson, Ian. *La represión nacionalista de Granada en 1936, y la muerte de Federico García Lorca.* Paris: Ruedo Ibérico, 1971.

*Giménez Caballero, Ernesto. *Lengua y literatura de España y su Imperio.* Madrid: 1953.

*Guillén, Jorge. *Federico en persona; semblanza y epistolario.* Buenos Aires: Emecé Editoris SA, 1959.

Honig, Edwin. *García Lorca.* Norfolk: New Directions, 1944.

Llafranque, Marie. *Federico García Lorca; Textes et Propos de Lorca, Points de vue critiques; Temoignages.* Paris: Editions Seghers, 1966.

Llafranque, Marie. *Les Idées Esthetiques de Federico García Lorca.* Bordeaux: Institut d'études Hispaniques, 1967.

Lima, Robert A. *The Theater of García Lorca.* New York: Las Americas Publishing Co., 1963.

Martínez Nadal, Rafael. *El Público, Amor y Muerte en la Obra de Federico García Lorca.* Mexico City: Joaquín Mortiz, 1975.

*Martínez Nadal, Rafael. *El Público, Amor, Teatro y Caballos en la Obra de Federico García Lorca.* Oxford: The Dolphin Book Co., Ltd., 1970.

*Moreno Villa, José. *Vida en Claro.* Mexico City: El Colegio de Mexico, 1944.

*Morla Lynch, Carlos. *En España con Federico García Lorca (páginas de un diario íntimo. 1928–36).* Madrid: Aguilar SA de Ediciones, 1957.

*Nadeau, Maurice. *History of Surrealism.* Translated by Richard Howard. New York: Macmillan, 1965.

Schonberg, Jean-Louis. *Federico García Lorca; l'Homme, l'Oeuvre.* Paris: Librarie Plon, 1956.

*Prieto Muñoz, Gregorio. *García Lorca as a Painter.* London: The De la More Press, 1967.

Trend, John Brand. *Lorca and the Spanish Poetic Tradition.* New York: Oxford University Press, 1946.

Trend, John Brand. *Federico García Lorca.* Cambridge: L. I. Severs Ltd., 1957.

Trend, John Brand. *Manuel de Falla and Spanish Music.* New York: Alfred A. Knopf, 1929.

Trend, John Brand. *A Picture of Modern Spain: Men and Music.* London: Constable and Co., Ltd., 1921.